Photo by Charlaine Brown

A scene from the South Coast Repertory production of "Abundance." Set design by Adrianne Lobel.

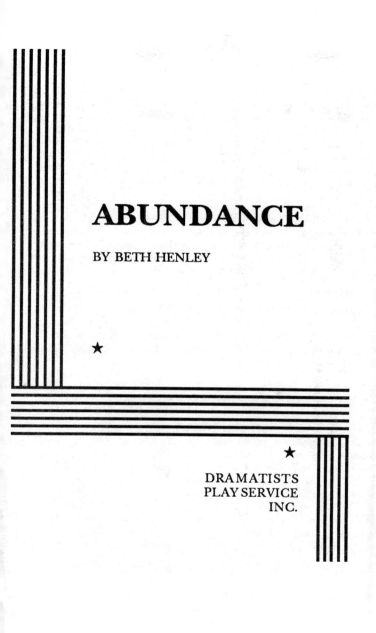

# ABUNDANCE

BY BETH HENLEY

DRAMATISTS
PLAY SERVICE
INC.

ABUNDANCE
Copyright © 1991, Beth Henley

All Rights Reserved

## SPECIAL NOTE

Anyone receiving permission to produce ABUNDANCE is required to give credit to the Author as sole and exclusive Author of the Play on the title page of all programs distributed in connection with performances of the Play and in all instances in which the title of the Play appears for purposes of advertising, publicizing or otherwise exploiting the Play and/or a production thereof. The name of the Author must appear on a separate line, in which no other name appears, immediately beneath the title and in size of type equal to 50% of the size of the largest, most prominent letter used for the title of the Play. No person, firm or entity may receive credit larger or more prominent than that accorded the Author.

## SPECIAL NOTE ON ORIGINAL MUSIC

A tape (and cue sheet) containing the original music composed by Michael Roth for the New York production of the Play is available through the Play Service. There is an additional royalty of $10.00 per performance for the use of this music.

*Dedicated to Robert Darnell
and the spirit of Darnelli Points*

ABUNDANCE was produced by the Manhattan Theatre Club (Lynne Meadow, Artistic Director; Barry Grove, Managing Director) in New York City on October 4, 1990. It was directed by Ron Lagomarsino; the set design was by Adrianne Lobel; the costume design was by Robert Wojewodski; the lighting design was by Paulie Jenkins; music and sound were by Michael Roth; the fight director was J. Allen Suddeth; and the production stage manager was Ruth Kreshka. The cast was as follows:

BESS JOHNSON.................................................Amanda Plummer
MACON HILL ..............................................................Tess Harper
JACK FLAN ...........................................................Michael Rooker
WILLIAM CURTIS..................................................Lanny Flaherty
ELMORE CROME ....................................................Keith Reddin

ABUNDANCE was produced by the South Coast Repertory (David Emmes, Producing Artistic Director; Martin Benson, Artistic Director), Costa Mesa, California, on April 21, 1989. It was directed by Ron Lagomarsino; the set design was by Adrianne Lobel; the costume design was by Robert Wojewodski; the lighting design was by Paulie Jenkins; music and sound were by Michael Roth; and the production manager was Paul Hammond. The cast was as follows:

BESS JOHNSON..........................................................O-Lan Jones
MACON HILL............................................................Belita Moreno
JACK FLAN ................................................................Bruce Wright
WILLIAM CURTIS ..............................................Jimme Ray Weeks
ELMORE CROME ......................................................John Walcutt

## CAST OF CHARACTERS

BESS JOHNSON
MACON HILL
JACK FLAN
WILLIAM CURTIS
PROFESSOR ELMORE CROME

## TIME

The play spans twenty-five years, starting in the late 1860's.

## PLACE

Wyoming Territory and later in St. Louis, Missouri.

# ABUNDANCE

## ACT I

### Scene 1

*Late 1860's. Morning. Spring.*

*Outside a stagecoach ranché in the Wyoming Territory.*

*Bess Johnson, a young woman, sits on a bench. There is a bag at her feet. She wears a dirty travelling suit that has no buttons.*

BESS. *(Singing to herself.)* Roses love sunshine
Violets love dew
Angels in heaven
Know I love you.

Build me a castle forty
   feet high
So I can see him as he
   rides by
*(Bess stops singing and speaks softly to herself.)* The size of the sky. The size of the sky. *(Macon Hill enters wearing green goggles and a cape. She is covered with road dust and carries a satchel and green biscuits on a platter. She is whistling. She stops when she sees Bess.)*
MACON. Lord Almighty.
BESS. What?
MACON. You're like me.
BESS. Huh?
MACON. Sure. You're like me. Biscuit?
BESS. Please.
MACON. Go ahead. Help yourself. What's mine is yours; what's yours is mine. After all, you're like me. You've come out

west to see the elephant. Hey, true or no?

BESS. Elephant. No.

MACON. To see what's out there; whatever's out there. *(Beat.)* What do you guess is out there?

BESS. Don't know.

MACON. Right. Could be anything. I savor the boundlessness of it all. The wild flavor. I'm drunk with western fever. Have you ever seen a map of the world?

BESS. Uh huh.

MACON. Well, it stopped my heart. There are oceans out there. Oceans aplenty, and I swear to you I'm gonna see one and walk in one and swim in one for sure. I love water, it never stops moving. I want to discover gold and be rich. I want to erect an ice palace and kill an Indian with a hot bullet. I'm ready for some sweeping changes. How about you? We could be friends throughout it all. It's part of our destiny. I can smell destiny. One day I'm gonna write a novel about it all and put you in it. What's your name? *(Macon produces a pad and pencil.)*

BESS. Bess Johnson.

MACON. *(Writing down the name.)* Good. That's a good name for a novel. Bess Johnson. Will you be my friend?

BESS. It'd be a pleasure. A true pleasure. Could I — could I trouble you for another biscuit?

MACON. Why sure. Sure, I hate stinginess. You'll never get anywhere watching every egg, nickel and biscuit. Ya gotta let it go! Let it go! Go! And I don't give a damn if ya never pay me back.

BESS. Thanks kindly. I'm near pined t'death with famine. These green biscuits taste heaven to me.

MACON. Why, how long ya been at the ranché?

BESS. Ten days, I been waiting here. My travel money's all spent. Yesterday I traded French Pete my buttons for an extra night's lodging. I'm at my rope's end if Mr. Flan don't get here real soon; I don't know what.

MACON. Who's Mr. Flan?

BESS. He's the man who's coming t'pick me up. We're to be wed.

8

MACON. Wed? A wedding?

BESS. That's right. It's been arranged.

MACON. Then you're a bride-to-be?

BESS. Yeah.

MACON. Lord Almighty! Angels sing; devils dance! I'm a bride-to-be, too. It's like I said, you're like me. It's true! It's true! Tell me, do ya know your husband or is he a stranger to ya?

BESS. We had ... correspondence.

MACON. Correspondence. Me too. And he sent you the fare?

BESS. Partial.

MACON. Me too! Me too! (She whistles a few notes.) Ya know what I hope? I hope our husbands don't turn out t'be just too damn ugly t'stand.

BESS. You think they'll be ugly?

MACON. Maybe. Maybe. But I hear divorce is cheap and easily obtainable out here in the west.

BESS. I'd never get no divorce.

MACON. Honey, I'd rip the wings off an angel if I thought they'd help me fly! You may find this hard to believe, but back home they considered me the runt of the family. See, those folks are all full, large-bodied people, and to them I appeared to be some sort of runt. But out here I can be whoever I want. Nobody knows me. I'm gonna make everything up as I go. It's gonna be a whole new experience. We're dealing with the lure of the unknown. Yeah, we're hunting down the elephant! Bang! Bang! Bang! What's wrong with you? You're looking morose.

BESS. I — I'm just hoping my husband ain't gonna be real terrible ugly.

MACON. Well, Bess, I hope so too.

BESS. It don't mention nothing about his looks in the matrimonial ad.

MACON. Well, now that ain't good news. Folks generally like t'feature their good qualities in them advertisements.

BESS. 'Course I know I'm no prize. I got nice hair, but my eyes are too close together and my nerves are somewhat aggravated. Still, I was hoping we'd be in love like people in them stories. The ones about princesses and chimney sweeps and dragon slayers.

MACON. Oh, them stories ain't true. They ain't factual. Catapult them stories out of your brain. Do it! Do it! Catapult 'em!

BESS. I don't know, I — well, I bet he's gonna like me some.

MACON. Sure. Maybe he'll be cordial at Christmas.

BESS. I promise I'll be a good wife, patient and submissive. If only he'd come. I hope he ain't forgotten. He sent partial fare. Three letters and partial fare. Three letters all about the size of the western sky.

MACON. Damn! What size is it?

BESS. The largest he has witnessed.

MACON. Glory be.

BESS. And he loves singing. I can sing real pretty. Oh, I'm betting we're gonna be a match made in heaven, if only I ain't left stranded. See, 'cause, well, I don't know how I'll get by. I can't do nothing. I don't know nothing. I oughta know something by now. I went t'school. They must have taught me something there. But I can't even recall what my favorite color is. Maybe it's blue, but I'm just guessing.

MACON. Well, the fact is, if ya know too much, it's just gonna limit your thinking. Take me, I got this brown dress and I don't even get upset about it 'cause I got no recollection in my mind that my favorite color is blue. I mean, it may be, but I don't know it. Have another biscuit.

BESS. It's your last one.

MACON. I saved it for you. *(Jack Flan enters. He is handsome, with an air of wild danger.)*

JACK. 'Morning.

MACON. 'Morning.

JACK. I'm looking for — Is one of you Bess Johnson?

BESS. That's me. That's me. I'm here. I'm here. That's me.

JACK. Uh huh.

BESS. Are you Mr. Michael Flan?

JACK. No, I'm Jack Flan, Mike's brother.

BESS. Oh well, well, pleased t'meet you, Mr. Jack Flan. Would you do me the great favor of taking me t'meet Mr. Michael Flan?

JACK. Mike's dead.

BESS. What?

JACK. Got killed in an accident and died.

BESS. Are you saying Mr. Michael Flan is no longer living?

JACK. That's right; he's dead.

BESS. Dead. Oh my. Oh my. Lord, Lord, Lord.

JACK. What's wrong with you? You never laid eyes on him. You're just some stranger.

MACON. Hey, hey, don't be so grim.

BESS. *(Crying with fury.)* I wanna go home. I'll die if I stay here. I don't wanna die in this miserable, filthy territory!

JACK. Look at her crying. She's a woman alright.

BESS. Oh, how can this be? My husband's dead. He's gone. He's dead. I never even got to meet him or shake his hand or say, "I do." "I do, I do." I worked on saying them words the whole way here. Over cliffs, across streams, in the rain, in the dust. "I do, I do." Every dream I ever had I said in them words. "I do, I do, I do, I do..."

JACK. I'm gonna knock her down.

MACON. Don't do that. *(Jack shoves Macon aside, then goes and knocks down Bess. Macon comes at him with a knife. He takes her by the hair and slings her to the ground.)*

JACK. *(To Macon.)* You're out west now. Things are different here. *(To Bess.)* Come on with me. I'm gonna marry you. But I won't have you crying. Never again. You got that clear?

BESS. Yes.

JACK. Let's go. *(They exit. Macon gets to her feet.)*

MACON. That was something. I didn't mind that. That was something. *(Macon whistles to herself. William Curtis enters. He is neatly dressed. He wears a patch over the left eye. There is a scar down the same side of his face.)*

WILL. Hello. Are you Miss Macon Hill?

MACON. Yes, I am.

WILL. I'm Mr. William Curtis. I've come for you. You're to be my wife.

MACON. Well, here I am. I'm ready to ride. *(They exit.)*

### End of Scene 1

11

## Scene 2

*Later that day.*

*Jack's cabin. Jack sits in a chair. Bess is pulling filth-covered blankets off the floor.*

BESS.  This is a beautiful home. Some women get squeamish over fleas and ticks and lice, not me. We'll root 'em out by bathing with plenty of sheep-dip and then we'll add kerosene to the sheep-dip and boil all our clothes and bedding in the sheep-dip and kerosene. That'll root 'em out. Kill 'em all for sure. I'm gonna be happy here. I can feel it coming.

JACK.  Don't start messing with things around here. That's not my way.

BESS.  Uh huh. Uh huh.

JACK.  *(A beat.)* I'm not used to you being here.

BESS.  *(A beat.)* I can — I can cook something.

JACK.  There's nothing t'cook. Got some dried beef on the shelf.

BESS.  I'll fetch it. *(She gets the dried beef and brings it back to the table.)* Here.

JACK.  Thanks.

BESS.  Welcome. You're welcome. *(They chew on the dried beef in silence.)* Mr. Flan.

JACK.  Yeah?

BESS.  Do you like singing?

JACK.  No. *(A beat.)*

BESS.  Your brother said he liked singing.

JACK.  You never met my brother.

BESS.  He wrote it in his letters.

JACK.  That he liked singing?

BESS.  Yes.

JACK.  Never said nothing to me about it.

BESS.  I got his letters, if ya wanna look at 'em. *(Jack nods.)* Here they are. He wrote three of 'em. *(Jack takes the letters and looks at all three of them.)* In each one of 'em he mentions something about singing. Says there's not much music out

12

here, but for the birds. I was hoping to change things for him. See, me, well, I sing — *(Jack tosses down the letters.)* Pretty letters, ain't they?

JACK. I don't read writing.

BESS. Oh, well, I could read 'em for ya. *(Bess picks up one of the letters and starts to read it.)* "Dear Miss Bess Johnson, I was overjoyed to receive your correspondence accepting my humble proposal of marriage. I sincerely believe you will not be disappointed living in the west. The skies out here are the largest I have witnessed. The stars hang so low you feel you could reach up and touch them with your hand — " *(Jack grabs the letter out of her hand. He tears up the letters.)*

JACK. Hey! You don't read t'me! I ain't no baby. You ain't no schoolmarm. You got that clear?! Nobody reads me nothing! Nothing! Nothing at all!

BESS. *(Overlapping.)* Don't tear 'em! Please, don't tear 'em!

JACK. I did! I tore 'em! They're torn! And I don't want you singing. There'll be no singing. I don't tolerate no singing never. You hear me?

BESS. I do.

JACK. Hey, you better not start crying. Remember what I warned you about crying?

BESS. I won't. I won't never be crying. I'm telling ya. I can do things right.

### End of Scene 2

### Scene 3

*Same day.*

*William's cabin. Will and Macon enter.*

WILL. Come on in. Here we are.

MACON. I see.

WILL. What do you mean by that, Miss Hill?

MACON. Nothing. I just see — Here we are.

WILL. I lost it in a mining accident.

MACON. What?

WILL. No need playing coy. I see you see it's missing.

MACON. Oh, your eye.

WILL. Yeah.

MACON. Oh, well, I did observe it'd been removed.

WILL. Man knocked it out with a mining pick. It was an honest mistake. There was no violence or malice intended.

MACON. Hmm. Well, I bet you wish it didn't happen.

WILL. I intend to order a glass one just as soon as finances permit. It'll be brown, same color as the one I have left.

MACON. Uh huh.

WILL. You can tell me right now if this makes a difference. I'll send you back if it does.

MACON. I ain't going back.

WILL. Alright. *(Pause.)* Miss Hill?

MACON. Yeah?

WILL. I got something for you.

MACON. What?

WILL. It's a ring. A ruby ring. *(He takes out a ring.)*

MACON. Oh, I cherish rings.

WILL. It was my wife's.

MACON. Your wife's.

WILL. Yes, she died.

MACON. Oh.

WILL. Last winter. It was snowing. *(Pause.)* She once had a photograph taken of her. Would you like to see it?

MACON. Alright.

WILL. *(He hands her a photograph.)* Her name was Barbara Jane.

MACON. What'd she die from?

WILL. No one could say for sure. She took to bed. A long time I stood by her. One night she coughed up both her lungs. There was nothing to be done.

MACON. She looks pretty sickly.

WILL. I thought she was beautiful.

MACON. Well, I don't think I want her ring.

14

WILL. Why not?

MACON. Could have her sickness on it. I don't want no part of it.

WILL. She never wore the ring when she was sick. She only wore it the first year of our marriage.

MACON. Why's that?

WILL. She lost three fingers in a sheep-shearing accident. One of 'em was the ring finger.

MACON. Well, y'all certainly seem t'be plagued with all sorts of disfiguring misfortunes around here.

WILL. If the ring won't do, I'll get a piece of tin and bend it around for ya. Maybe in time I can get ya another ring with a stone in it.

MACON. I'd appreciate it.

WILL. The Marrying Squire will be here at the end of the month. At that time we'll be wed.

MACON. Uh huh. *(They glance at each other, then turn away in silence.)*

### End of Scene 3

### Scene 4

*Three months later. A summer's night. In a field. Bess is calling out to Macon who has disappeared into the night.*

BESS. Macon! Macon, you out there? Where are you? Where'd you go? Indians could be lurking! Come back! Macon! *(Macon runs onstage, breathless with excitement.)*

MACON. I almost touched it!

BESS. I thought you was lost in the dark.

MACON. I almost did.

BESS. Indians might a' captured you.

MACON. From the top of that far-off hill I almost felt it.

BESS. What?

15

MACON. That little silver star. The one sitting there so low in the sky. See it?

BESS. Uh-huh.

MACON. Stars send off chills. Closer you get, the more chill you feel. Go on try it. Go on, reach up for it. *(Bess reaches up to touch a star.)* There you go! Jump! Jump! Did ya feel the chill?

BESS. Maybe I might a' felt some sort of small chill.

MACON. The thing we gotta look out for is a falling star. You ever seen a falling star?

BESS. No.

MACON. Well, now, when we see one of them, we gotta run for it. I know I can touch one of them. *(Macon whistles.)*

BESS. That's a nice tune. I never heard it.

MACON. It's a good song. You wanna learn it?

BESS. Oh, I don't sing no more. Jack don't like it.

MACON. Jack don't like singing?

BESS. His brother, Michael, liked singing. But Jack don't. *(Macon whistles a moment.)*

MACON. I don't mean t'speak out, but your husband, well, he don't seem t'got a whole lot to recommend him.

BESS. Oh, he suits me fine. Why, I ain't sure we ain't a match made in heaven. Soon as we get the inheritance money Mr. Michael Flan left. Everything'll be rosy.

MACON. Well, I sure hope things work out for you. I got doubts about my own predicament.

BESS. Don't ya get on with your new husband? He seems a good man t'me.

MACON. Well, I hate to criticize Mr. Curtis. I know he does try; but, well, frankly, I'm allergic to him physically.

BESS. Is it 'cause of his eye?

MACON. Could be part of it. But even with one more eye, I might find him repulsive. *(Macon whistles.)*

BESS. Show me how t'do that.

MACON. What? Whistle?

BESS. Yeah.

MACON. Easiest thing in the world. Just watch me. I'll show ya how. *(Macon whistles. Bess tries to imitate her. She fails. Macon*

*starts to laugh.)*
BESS.  I can't get it!
MACON.  You will!
BESS.  When?
MACON.  Soon! *(Running off.)* Come on! I wanna show you the white jasmine. They're in bloom now down by the pond. *(They exit.)*

### End of Scene 4


### Scene 5

*Three months later. Autumn.*

*Jack is walking down a path near his property. He carries a load of mining equipment. He sees something coming. He hides behind a rock. Macon appears carrying a bundle. She wears a cape and is whistling. Jack takes out his six-shooter, aims it at Macon and fires. Macon screams in horror and throws the bundle up in the air.*

MACON.  Aah! *(Jack saunters out from behind the rock brandishing the pistol.)* You trying to kill me?!
JACK.  If I was, you'd be dead. *(A beat.)* Better watch out. Bullets make me smile. *(Jack shoots off the gun and then exits. Macon stands frozen with fear and fury. Bess enters.)*
BESS.  Macon, you alright?
MACON.  Yeah. It was Jack. He seen a snake.
BESS.  He kill it?
MACON.  Scared it away. Here, I got two small items for ya. Coffee and some shoes.
BESS.  Thank you, Macon, but I don't need t'take things from you no more. Me and Jack, well, everything has turned around.
MACON.  You talking on account of Lockwood's mine?
BESS.  That's right. Jack purchased it last night with all the

17

inheritance money Mr. Michael Flan left. It's sugared with pure gold like a town of fairies been dancing there. *(Macon whistles for a moment, then stops.)*

MACON. Pause a moment, Bess. Use the round thing above your shoulders and tell me why anyone in this world would sell a mine laden with pure gold?

BESS. — Mr. Lockwood's very old. His eyesight's poor.

MACON. Well, his mind is sharp.

BESS. What're you telling?

MACON. I know that mine. It's dry as a parched tongue. Lockwood salted that claim with gold dust just to lead greedy fools astray.

BESS. I hope that ain't so. 'Cause we paid him for it. We paid him all we had. Oh, what's gonna become of us now? Times is already harder than hard.

MACON. I know. I seen it coming. Now's it's arriving at the front door.

BESS. Not at your door. Things are going good for you and Will Curtis.

MACON. Maybe in your eyes you see it that way. But me, I've come to a staunch conclusion. We gotta go. We gotta go now. We could leave here tonight.

BESS. Where'd we go?

MACON. West. We'd be going west.

BESS. Which way west?

MACON. Out past the Jack pine and yellow cedar, off through the grass that grows scarlet red across the plains, and on and on and onward.

BESS. We'd die of thirst and famine.

MACON. We'll drink plentiful before starting out, then chew constantly on small sticks to help prevent parching. Wild fruits grow all in abundance. Ripe plums will cool our fevered lips.

BESS. What about the Indians?

MACON. I got a cup of cayenne pepper and a corn knife t'take care of 'em. Whatever happens. It don't matter. Why limit the limitless. I'll write a novel about it all and put you in it. Go with me.

BESS. I can't go.

MACON. Why not?

BESS. I'm married.

MACON. He don't treat ya no good.

BESS. I'll learn t'make him.

MACON. You can't change his nature.

BESS. I'm here to try. You go on. You go without me. Please. Ya don't need me.

MACON. You're my one friend.

BESS. I ain't special.

MACON. You looked my way.

BESS. I can't go. I gave out my oath.

MACON. (A beat.) Here's the coffee. It's from parched corn and sorghum sweetening, but better than the dried carrot variety you been drinking. And take these shoes; those flaps of skin will never get you through the winter.

BESS. I'll pay ya back someday.

MACON. Don't mention it. I like giving gifts. It's who I am.

### End of Scene 5

### Scene 6

*A year later. Fall.*

*A clearing.*

WILL. (Offstage.) Hey, let go of that wood! You ain't stealing no more of my wood!

JACK. (Offstage.) Stealing? I ain't stealing nothing! (A crack of wood offstage.) Ow! (Jack is thrown onstage.)

WILL. I'll kill you, you son of a bitch!

JACK. You calling me a thief?

WILL. That's my wood. Pay me for it fair.

JACK. Miser.

WILL. Shiftless.

JACK. Blind mouse, one-eyed, scar-faced farmer —

WILL. *(Overlapping.)* Lazy, no-good, fool's gold miner — *(Jack and Will tear into each other. The fight is brutal. Macon enters. She carries a walking stick and wears field glasses around her neck. She dives into the fight, knocking the men apart with her stick.)*

MACON. Hey, hey, what's going on here? Stop it! Please! Hey! We're all neighbors here. Will Curtis, what is wrong?

WILL. He wants to freeload more of our wood. Hasn't paid me for the last five bundles. He ain't getting nothing else for free.

MACON. Will. Please! There's a bobcat caught in the trap line. Better go check on it before it gets loose. I don't want it on our hands.

WILL. *(To Jack.)* You get off my place. *(Will exits.)*

JACK. Good thing he went off. I might a' had t'kill him.

MACON. You come here looking for wood? *(Jack looks away from her.)* You know where the woodpile is. You take some and haul it on home.

JACK. Just so you'll know, I got things in the works; irons in the fire. Nothing worries me.

MACON. You oughta look to salted pork. Last year we put up 1,560 pounds at three-and-a-half cents a pound.

JACK. It don't interest me. I'd rather gamble for the high stakes. 'Afternoon, May Ann.

MACON. What?

JACK. May Ann. It's a prettier name than Macon. Its suits you better. I think I'll call you that.

MACON. Tell Bess she can keep the needle she borrowed. I won't need it back till Monday.

JACK. Uh huh.

MACON. She's had a hard summer, losing that baby. You need t'watch after her.

JACK. Is that what I need? Is that what I need, May Ann?

MACON. That's not my name.

JACK. It is to me. *(Jack exits. Macon pauses a moment, then looks after Jack through the field glasses. Will enters.)*

WILL. Bobcat got loose. Chewed off its paw. *(Macon quickly stops looking through the field glasses.)*

MACON. Will.

WILL. What?

MACON. I told him t'take some wood.

WILL. You what?

MACON. All they got t' burn is green twigs.

WILL. I don't like that, Macon. Why, that man's a freeloading ne'er-do-well. We don't want nothing to do with him.

MACON. Still I gotta look out for Bess. She's a friend of mine.

WILL. I don't understand about her and you. She's not special. Just some joyless creature with sawdust for brains.

MACON. Don't say that.

WILL. Look, I've observed in her strong symptoms of derangement that just ain't healthy. That ain't right.

MACON. Don't you got one drop of human kindness inside your whole bloodstream. It was just last summer she buried her infant child in a soap box under a prickly pear tree and wolves dug it up for supper.

WILL. Things haven't gone her way, that's true. Still, I cannot agree with her strange and gruesome behavior. How she dresses up that prairie dog of hers in a calico bonnet and shawl; sits there rocking it on the porch, talking to it just like it was a somebody.

MACON. People do strange things t'get by.

WILL. That may be. But everybody's got to make their own way. If they drop down, it ain't for you to carry them. (*Macon turns away from him and looks through the field glasses into the distance.*) I just don't like being exploited. I don't like the exploitation. People should earn what they get. What're you looking at?

MACON. Checking the cows.

WILL. How're the cows? Can you see the cows?

MACON. I see 'em.

WILL. Anyway, what's a load of wood? After all, we seem to be prospering. Last year we sold 1,560 pounds of salt pork at three-and-a-half cents a pound. Friday I'll go into town and see if the copper kettle you ordered from St. Louis has been delivered in the mail. After all, they're the ones with problems and burdens. If their luck doesn't change, they won't make it through the winter. They'll starve to death by Christmas. When the copper kettle comes, it will improve the looks of our cabin. You spoke about it before. You said it would add cheerfulness.

**End of Scene 6**

**Scene 7**

*Christmas, months later. Night.*

*Jack's cabin. It is snowing. The wind is howling. Jack sits staring. Bess is on the floor, picking shreds of wheat out of the straw mattress.*

BESS. You know what, Jack? Jack, you know what? I think it's Christmas. I've been thinking that all day.
JACK. I don't know.
BESS. I could be wrong. But I might be right. There's not much wheat in all this straw. Not much wheat to speak of. Would you agree it could be Christmas?
JACK. Where's the prairie dog?
BESS. Of course, Macon would have been here by now if it'd been Christmas. She was planning to bring us a galore of a spread. I was looking forward to it. Maybe the bad weather's put her off. The blizzards. Blinding blizzards for weeks now. Keeping Christmas from our front door. Jack, something happened to Prairie Dog.
JACK. It did?
BESS. It was when you went out trying to kill us something this morning.
JACK. Yeah.
BESS. This man came by. Some wandering sort of vagabond dressed in rags. Dirt rags. He wanted a handout. Food, you know.
JACK. We don't have anything.

BESS. I told him. I sent him on his way. "We don't have anything," I said. "I gotta go through the straw in the bed mattress picking out slivers of wheat so we won't starve here to death. I don't have food to spare some unknown wanderer." He asked me for just a cup of warm water, but I said no. Not because we couldn't spare it, but just because I didn't want him around here on the premises anymore. Something about him. His face was red and dirty. His mouth was like a hole. (*About the wheat.*) This is not gonna be enough for supper, this right here.

JACK. So what happened to the dog?

BESS. As he, as the vagabond was leaving, Prairie Dog followed after him barking. He picked up a stone and grabbed her by the throat and beat her head in with it. With the rock. She's out back in a flour sack. I'd burn her to ashes, if only we could spare the wood.

JACK. This is your fault.

BESS. Yes it it.

JACK. You're so weak. You make me sick. Christ, you're useless. I may just have to kill you.

BESS. You know what? I think it is Christmas. It's Christmas, after all. And you know what? I got something for you. I been saving it for Christmas. A surprise for you. A present. A Christmas gift. I been hoarding it away for you, but the time has come. The day has arrived. Merry Christmas, Jack. (*She produces a sack of cornmeal.*)

JACK. What is that?

BESS. Cornmeal.

JACK. Cornmeal. What're you gonna do with that?

BESS. Make you some cornbread. Cornbread for Christmas. A surprise.

JACK. Yeah. Yeah, a real big surprise. Boo! Surprise! Boo!

BESS. It's special. It's a treat. Hot cornbread. A lot better than that ash-baked bread we used to have.

JACK. Yeah, sure. But I ain't gonna choke t'death on no ash-baked bread. I ain't gonna turn blue and purple and green till I die eating no ash-baked bread.

BESS. You ain't gonna die eating no cornbread neither.

JACK. You tell that to Mike. You tell that to my brother, Mike, who had himself a big hunk of cornbread and choked t'death on it while riding bareback over the swinging bridge.

BESS. I never knew about that. I never knew how he died. I swear it, I didn't.

JACK. You might not have known it. Possibly you never was told it. But I bet you guessed it. I bet you dreamed it up. First Mike, then the baby, next Prairie Dog, now me. You want us all dead, don't you? You like things dead. You want it all for yourself. Well, here, have it. Take it. *(He throws a handful of cornmeal in her face.)*

BESS. No —

JACK. *(He continues throwing the cornmeal at her.)* There. There you go.

BESS. Stop.

JACK. Take it all!

BESS. I wanted this to be good. I wanted to be your true one.

### End of Scene 7

### Scene 8

*Same night.*

*Will's cabin. Macon and Will are drinking cordials. It is Christmas.*

MACON. I don't think so, Mr. Curtis. I don't believe so in the slightest. We're in no agreement, whatsoever.

WILL. Reliance on one crop is too risky. I'll say no more.

MACON. I'm telling you wheat promises the largest cash return and there's nothing comparable to it.

WILL. Besides there're other cautions to attend. We don't wanna expand too rapidly. We oughtn't get ahead of ourselves.

MACON. But there's no way to get ahead of ourselves. Not with the Union Pacific track-laying crew coming through. We gotta look to the future. Did I steer you wrong about the pork prices? No, I did not. We bought up Dan Raymond's east field with the profits from salt pork. Turn that over in your head a minute.

WILL. Listen here —

MACON. Ssh! Ssh. Just turn it over. Churn it around. Let it fester. Here, now, I'll pour both of us another cordial. After all, it's Christmas. *(She pours out two drinks.)*

WILL. You have a nice way of pouring that drink. It looks delicate.

MACON. It's got a pretty color. The liquor.

WILL. Macon.

MACON. Huh?

WILL. There's, there's something for you. St. Nicholas left it, I guess. *(He hands her a gift with a card. She starts to open it.)*

MACON. A present for me.

WILL. Wait, wait. There's a card. Read the card.

MACON. Oh, yeah. "Merry Christmas, Mrs. Curtis. You are sweet as honey. From Brown Spot." Brown Spot?

WILL. *(He laughs.)* Yeah.

MACON. Brown Spot, the cow?

WILL. She's your favorite one, ain't she?

MACON. Not really, I prefer Whitey.

WILL. Oh, oh, well, pretend it was from Whitey. It was supposed to be from Whitey. Alright, now open the gift. But first, tell me, what do you guess it's gonna be?

MACON. I don't know. I'm hoping for a thing.

WILL. I got a feeling it's what you're hoping for. *(She opens the gift.)* Well?

MACON. What is it?

WILL. It's an eye. A glass eye. It's brown, see?

MACON. Oh, yeah.

WILL. I promised you I'd get one and I've kept that promise. Want me to put it in?

MACON. Alright.

WILL. I need a looking glass. *(He goes to put in the eye.)* I tried it on before, right when it arrived. I been saving it five weeks now. It ain't real ... *(He groans.)* ... comfortable, but it makes a difference in my appearance. I think you'll appreciate it. *(He turns to her, wearing the eye.)* Hello.

MACON. Hi.

WILL. What do you think? Looks pretty real, huh?

MACON. Uh-huh.

WILL. If it wasn't for the scar, no one could guess which was real and which was glass.

MACON. Don't it hurt inside there?

WILL. Sure, but that's part of it. I'll adjust. Give me another cordial. That'll help it. *(Macon pours him another drink.)* I like to watch that pouring. Your hands. Delicate. *(She brings him the drink and starts to leave. He gently holds her arm.)* Say here. *(He drinks the drink.)* Macon, I know most times you don't feel like being nice to me. But I thought tonight, since I got this new eye, maybe you would.

MACON. *(A beat.)* Alright. *(Macon unbuttons her top and takes it off.)* Mr. Curtis?

WILL. Yes?

MACON. Have you thought any more about planting wheat in the east field?

WILL. Not much.

MACON. It'd be a good idea.

WILL. Alright, if that's what you think. We'll do it that way. *(There is a loud, desperate knocking at the door.)*

BESS. *(Offstage.)* Macon! Macon, let me in. Please. Let me in. Please, please. *(Macon rushes to the door. Bess enters. She wears a thin coat. She is covered with snow, wheat and cornmeal. Frozen blood is caked to her forehead.)*

MACON. Bess, Bess, come in. Get in. Look at you. You've been hurt.

BESS. You've got to help. My husband Jack — he's in an insane condition.

MACON. She's freezing. Bring a blanket. My God. My God, Bess.

BESS. He took a torch and set our cabin on fire. It's burning hot, hot in the snow.

MACON. Will, we gotta go see to Jack Flan.

WILL. I'll see to him. I'll go. Both of you stay here. I'll

handle his derangement. *(Will exits.)*

MACON. Here, get outta these wet boots. How in the world did you get here? How did you cross the gulch in this blizzard and not freeze to death?

BESS. Freeze t'death. Freeze t'death. I like the sound of that prediction. I long for the flutter of angel's wings.

MACON. Calm down. You're in a fit of delirium. Let me wash off your face for you.

BESS. It's all uncoiling. The springs in my mind. In my body. They're all loose and jumping out. Rusted and twisted.

MACON. I should have come to you. I should have braved the storm. I had your Christmas spread all packed up, I just been waiting for a break in the weather.

BESS. I wish you'd come. I been so lonely. I been going outside and hugging icy trees, clinging to them like they was alive and could hold me back. I feel so empty sometimes I eat warm mud, trying to fill up the craving.

MACON. Hush now. You're with me now. Let me brush out your hair. You got straw and sticks in your hair.

BESS. I just wanna say — I just wanna say —

MACON. What?

BESS. Early disappointments are embittering my life.

MACON. I'll draw you a bath of herbs and water. Sleep will fall on you. It'll restore your peace.

BESS. Macon?

MACON. Huh?

BESS. Let's go west.

MACON. West?

BESS. Let's start all over. Let's start from scratch. See, I've tried and I've tried, but I'm starting to believe Jack, he's just not in my stars.

MACON. I have to say — I have to remember — I did, I always thought I'd make much more of myself than this. My husband gave me a Christmas card from our cow. Still, I need to think things out. There's a lot we don't know. Practical knowledge, reality, and facts.

BESS. But we will go?

MACON. Oh yes, we'll go. Soon we'll go.

27

BESS. I realize now — now that you're brushing my hair, that I love you so much more; so much more than anyone else.

### End of Scene 8

### Scene 9

*Over two years have passed. It is spring.*

*Outside Will's cabin. Bright sun shines down on Jack who is sitting on a fence eating a large piece of pound cake. He wears dress pants, but is barefoot and bare-chested. His hair is slicked back.*

*Will enters, barefoot and bare-chested. He carries two freshly pressed dress shirts.*

WILL. Here're the shirts.

JACK. Thanks.

WILL. It's gonna be some feast we're having; some celebration. *(Will puts on his shirt. Jack eats cake.)* Can you believe it's been four years since the Marrying Squire came through here and joined us all together in holy matrimony?

JACK. Happy anniversary.

WILL. I don't know. Time travels.

JACK. Well, what else can it do?

WILL. Yeah.... Have you checked into that new land that's opened up for homesteaders?

JACK. I hear there ain't nothing available that ain't worthless.

WILL. Huh. Well, have you given any more thought to rebuilding on your own property?

JACK. Everything's burnt up over there.

WILL. Then what're ya gonna do?

JACK. About what?

WILL. This is supposed to be the deadline. Our anniversary. We made a deal, remember? You and your wife could stay here until this anniversary, then your time was up.

JACK. Fine. Our time's up. Fine.

WILL. You have been living here over two years now. I know you was sick for a time, but we've been more than generous. That cabin's damn small.

JACK. All right, we'll go.

WILL. When?

JACK. Now. Right now.

WILL. Where're you gonna go?

JACK. Don't know. What do you care?

WILL. Well, don't go tonight. Wait a while more. Tonight's a celebration. Macon's been preparing all week. We best not spoil it.

JACK. Have it your way. *(Jack finishes the pound cake.)*

WILL. Was that the pound cake Macon brought out for us to sample?

JACK. Yeah. Damn good cake. Warm and moist, right outta the oven. *(Will hunts around for another piece of cake.)*

WILL. Where's my piece?

JACK. It's all gone.

WILL. She said she left a piece for me. She said she left two pieces.

JACK. Oh, well, I ate both of 'em.

WILL. Both of 'em. You ate both of 'em. But one of 'em was for me. One of 'em was my piece.

JACK. Sorry, I was hungry.

WILL. Well, damnation, I'm hungry, too! I'm hungry, too!

JACK. Look, you don't wanna ruin your supper. We're having a huge supper. It'd be a shame to spoil it.

WILL. Well, you didn't mind spoiling your supper. It didn't bother you none. Damn, I wish I had that cake.

JACK. Well, ya don't. It's gone. I hogged it. What can ya do?

WILL. Nothing. Just nothing. Not a damn thing.

JACK. Here, some crumbs. There's some crumbs left.

WILL. Forget it. I don't want it. Forget it. *(Will picks up some crumbs with his fingers and sticks them into his mouth.)*

**End of Scene 9**

## Scene 10

*Same day.*

*Inside Will's cabin. Bess wears a cape. She is walking around the room whistling and waving a list in the air. Macon sits at a table putting a waterfall hairpiece on her head.*

BESS. The list is complete. Completely complete. The day has arrived. The time has come. We have it all here: tallow, rice, tea, chip beef, grease bucket, water barrel, one kettle, one fry pan, powder, lead, shot — Check it out. See for yourself. The list is complete.

MACON. Do we have heavy rope?

BESS. Yes, we do. There it is right there.

MACON. And a tar bucket.

BESS. Tar bucket, tar bucket, right there. Right there. *(A beat.)* We should go tonight.

MACON. On our wedding anniversary?

BESS. Why drag things out?

MACON. It would be a cruel blow to our husbands, leaving them on our marriage day.

BESS. They'll adjust. They have each other.

MACON. I think we should wait a little.

BESS. It's just we've been waiting so long.

MACON. I wanna see what the pumpkin patch produces. I suspect, it's gonna yield a phenomenal crop.

BESS. I don't care about the pumpkins.

MACON. And I got that rainbow-colored petticoat ordered. I can't leave before it arrives. And next month I'm to be the judge of the baking contest. Last year I won first prize. I got t'stay here and judge. It's your duty if ya win first prize.

BESS. I got this feeling that you're putting me off. You swore last time soon as I got the new items on the list we'd go. Please, I can't stay here no longer.

MACON. Things aren't so bad for you now that you and Jack

have moved in here with us. You seem content most of the time.

BESS. I try not to show my hurt. I hide it in different parts of the house. I bury jars of it in the cellar; throw buckets of it down the well; iron streaks of it into the starched clothes and hang them in the closet. I just can't hide it no more. We got t'go now. You promised. You swore.

MACON. Stop pushing at me. I got things here. Out there, I don't know what. *(Jack enters wearing his clean shirt. He is still barefoot.)*

JACK. *(To Macon.)* Hi.

MACON. Hi.

JACK. Good pound cake.

MACON. Thanks.

JACK. Will's out there upset. Says I ate his piece a' cake.

MACON. I told you one was for him.

JACK. I was hungry.

MACON. Shame on you, Jack Flan. I'll go take this bowl out to him. He can lick the batter. *(Macon exits. There is a horrible moment of silence. Bess gets Jack's boots and takes them to him.)*

BESS. I polished your boots, Jack. *(Jack puts on a boot. Bess stands staring at the floor.)*

JACK. I can't see myself in the toe. *(Bess kneels down and slowly starts to shine the boot. Jack gives her a glance filled with cold-blooded disdain.)*

### End of Scene 10

### Scene 11

*That night.*

*Will's cabin, after the anniversary supper. Will, Macon, Jack and Bess are all gathered.*

JACK. Listen to me. I'm asking you. I'm making a point. Why do we have to be hungry? Why do we have to be hot or cold?

Why do we have to stink? If someone could find a cure, a potion, an elixir for one of these conditions or possibly all four of 'em, that person could make a whole lot of money. Picture a killing. Picture money to burn. The facts are simple. Nobody wants to stink. Not really. Not if they thought about it. They'd come to me; I'd give them the potion; they'd cross my palm with silver; thank you very much, next customer.

MACON.  It sounds like an exciting prospect.

JACK.  It's how my mind works.

WILL.  Well, he's right about one thing, nobody wants to stink.

BESS.  I know I don't. I used to put vanilla behind my ears, but Jack said I smelt like food.

JACK.  I'd love another piece of that delicious pound cake. It melts like butter in my mouth. *(Macon takes the last piece of cake and pushes it onto Jack's plate.)*

MACON.  Well, I'm delighted nothing's going to waste.

WILL.  Was that the last piece?

MACON.  *(Nods.)* Uh huh.

JACK.  *(Biting into the cake.)* Mmm, mmm. You cook better than anybody I ever knew.

MACON.  Thank you, Jack, but Bess helped out a lot.

BESS.  Not much really.

JACK.  She's good at scrubbing dishes, but all her cakes fall flat as nickels.

MACON.  Why, that's not true, Jack Flan. Why, that two-layer strawberry cake she made for my birthday was a sensation.

BESS.  Oh, no, Macon, you don't remember. It was a five-layer carrot cake I made for you, but it only rose half an inch high. We all got such a big laugh out of it.

MACON.  Oh, that's right. I remember now.

WILL.  Your wife sure is good for a laugh, I'll say that. Remember when she asked me, "How'd I get my eye t'grow back?" *(Everyone laughs.)* She thought this glass eye was a real eye that just sprouted back there in the socket like a radish.

JACK.  She's a howl alright.

BESS.  *(Cheerfully.)* I guess I've just been dreadfully stupid all my life.

MACON. Don't listen to them. They're only having fun. It's all foolishness. Why, no one's even noticed the bow in Bess's hair. Turn around, please. Now isn't that a lovely sight?

JACK. Yes, it is. She's got pretty hair. Her eyes are too close together. But she's got pretty hair. *(To Macon.)* What about you? Your hair looks different tonight. What happened to it?

MACON. Waterfall curls. I ordered them from Boston. They're the latest sensation.

JACK. Ain't they something.

WILL. Delicate.

JACK. Lovely, lovely, lovely.

BESS. The ribbon's my favorite color. It's blue. Macon lent it to me. It's her favorite color, too. We're alike, us two. *(Bess points to a bucket of daisies.)* Both of us love daisies. They're our favorite flower.

MACON. Oh, daisies aren't my favorite flower. My favorite flowers are tulips.

BESS. Tulips?

MACON. They grow in this small country called Holland. They're the most beautiful flowers in the world. Daisies don't compare. Why, daisies are really nothing more than common weeds.

BESS. Well, I'm sure, if I ever got to see a tulip, they'd be my favorite flower, too.

MACON. Maybe someday we'll all go over to Holland and pick rows and rows of tulips. That would be a time to remember. Filling our skirts with golden tulips and tossing 'em up in the sky! Ho! Oh, I feel like being boisterous, let's have some celebrating! I wanna dance!

JACK. Alright!

WILL. Go ahead!

BESS. *(Overlapping.)* Me too! Me too! I love to dance!

MACON. I have a step I know. It's from the quadrille. It's the latest dancing fashion.

JACK. Let's see it!

MACON. Everyone's gotta clap! *(Macon, Bess and Will all start clapping.)* Come on, get the rhythm going! That's good! Keep it going! Jack Flan, why aren't you clapping?

33

JACK. I don't do anything to music. I don't dance to it. I don't clap to it. I like to watch it, but I won't join it.

MACON. You are as ridiculous as ever, surely more so. Here, hold my combs for me. Hold them, silly. Hold my combs. *(Macon gives her hair combs to Jack. He holds them for her. To Will and Bess.)* Clap for me now. Louder, please! Louder! *(Macon does some fancy dance steps to the clapping.)*

BESS. Bravo! Bravo!

WILL. She's delicate! Look how delicate!

JACK. Look at her go! Swing them curls.

BESS. Oh, I wanna join in!

MACON. Come on, Bess! Take a turn! *(Bess starts dancing wildly.)* That's it! Go now! Wow! What a dancer!

WILL. Watch out! Watch out! Oh, let it ride! Yes sir, yes sir, let it ride! *(Bess kicks her foot up high and falls on her butt.)*

BESS. Oops!

MACON. Oh, well, that was good! That was good! Give her a hand!

BESS. I fell down. I can't do things right. I think I'm clumsy.

WILL. You took a spill alright. Up in the air you went and down again.

JACK. Try to be more ladylike. Everyone saw all your things under there.

MACON. Come on, take another spin.

BESS. I don't wanna dance anymore.

MACON. Come on. You can do it.

BESS. No, please, let me be.

MACON. Well, I know, why don't you sing for us?

BESS. I don't sing. You know I don't sing.

JACK. That's right. She told me when we got married that she never sang. Didn't you mention that the very first day we met?

BESS. That's right. At one time I did sing, but I don't anymore.

MACON. Well, if you sang once, you can sing again. Why, I believe I've even heard you singing when you wash the clothes.

BESS. Oh, that's not singing; that's more like humming.

MACON. Well, if you can hum, you can sing. Please, sing a

34

song for us. I'd like to hear it.

BESS. Can I, Jack?

JACK. I don't know, can you?

BESS. Well, I do remember this one tune.

MACON. Good, let's hear it. You're on stage now. The stage is set for your song. The curtain is rising on you. Welcome Bess Flan and her singing! *(Macon claps.)*

BESS. *(Singing.)*
Down in the valley
The valley so low
Hang your head over
Hear the wind blow
Hear the wind blow, dear
Hear the wind blow
Angels in Heaven
I love you so

Roses are blue, dear
Roses are blue
Roses are blue
They're so, so blue
Blue, real, real blue ...

MACON. That was wonderful.

BESS. I — I guess I've forgotten the song. Some of it. How it goes.

WILL. I know that song. I've heard it before. It didn't sound right.

MACON. Do you know another one?

JACK. She didn't know that one.

MACON. She knew most of it and she's got such a lovely voice.

JACK. I don't know a thing about singing, but it seems to me, if you're gonna sing a song, you need to know the words to the song you pick.

BESS. I used to know a lot of songs. I knew 'em all by heart. It's just I haven't sung ever since I come out here. It felt funny opening up my throat to sing. Like it was somebody else who was singing. Somebody else who wasn't me. I think I'm gonna go outside in the moonlight and pick some night-blooming jasmine out by the pond. Their fragrance draws me to 'em. The smell of 'em and the moonlight. *(Bess exits.)*

JACK. For no apparent reason, she seems to have lost her mind.

MACON. I think you hurt her feelings about her singing.

JACK. What? I did not. I didn't say anything against her singing except she should brush up on the words.

MACON. Maybe you should go see to her.

JACK. She don't want me to see to her.

MACON. Why not?

JACK. She's mad at me about her damn singing.

WILL. All the cake's gone, I suppose.

MACON. Yes.

WILL. My eye's burning. I'm ready to take it out for the evening. *(Macon starts for the door.)* Where're you going?

MACON. Out to see to her. *(Macon exits. Offstage.)* Bess ... Bess ... *(etc.)*

WILL. *(A beat.)* Think they'll be alright out there in the dark?

JACK. I don't know.

WILL. There're wild animals out there this time of night. Coyotes for sure. Bears and wolves.

JACK. Indians, maybe.

WILL. Macon! Macon! *(Will exits.)*

MACON. *(Offstage.)* What? Huh?

WILL. *(Offstage.)* Macon, come back in here. I'll get Bess. *(Jack gets up, goes and pours himself a drink. Macon enters. Jack looks at her, then downs the drink.)*

JACK. Whiskey?

MACON. No

JACK. *(Pouring himself another drink.)* Are you sure ... May Ann?

MACON. Don't you call me that. Ever.

JACK. Alright. Here're your combs back. I been holding them for you. Pretty combs. Lucky, too. Lucky to be running all through your hair.

MACON. Don't talk to me. Sit there and don't talk to me.

JACK. *(A beat.)* May Ann; May Ann; May Ann.

MACON. Shut up.

JACK. You been circulating in my head. All through my head. You're more vivid to me than any other thought. I can't get you outta here. Can't knock you out; can't drink you out; can't scream you out. Never, never. You always here.

MACON. Stop it. Don't do this. Stop it.

JACK. Can't you see that I am outta control of my feelings over you?

MACON. Look, I don't want anything to do with you. I got a husband, Will. You got a wife, Bess, who is my dearest friend of mine. I would never, ever imagine betraying her feelings. Never, ever, even if I did care for you, which I do not and never will and never could; 'cause in all honesty, there's absolutely not one thing about you I can bear to stand. You're mean and selfish and a liar and a snake; I spit on your grave, which can't get dug up fast enough and deep enough to suit me just fine.

JACK. *(A beat.)* Well, I just wanna know one thing. You tell me one thing. Why did you ask me to hold your combs for you? You chose me to hold your combs. You placed them in my hand. Why'd you do that? Huh?

MACON. Because I — You were standing there nearest to me, and I realized how I was afraid when I danced the combs would fly out of my hair and get lost in some faraway, far off corner of the room. You must know, I mean it is common knowledge, that you can have somebody hold your combs for you and still believe with your whole being and heart that you hate them and they're worse than bad, but you just need your combs held and they happen to be standing in arm's reach.

JACK. You certainly are talking a lot. Rambling on. Why's that?

MACON. I — I don't know. I'm just talking. I just feel like talking. I got this sensation that keeps on telling me that silence ain't safe.

JACK. Hush now.

MACON. No, I can't allow no silence 'cause then something real terrible's gonna happen. The world might stop moving and that could start the earth shaking and everything'll just fall into cracks and openings and horrible holes —

JACK. Just hush a moment.

MACON. No, I won't, I can't, the world will break open; the oceans will disappear; the sky will be gone; I won't; I can't; I won't —

JACK. Hush or I'll have to gag you.

MACON. It won't do no good. I'll still go on mumbling and moaning all under the gag.

JACK. Maybe then, I'll just have to break your neck. *(Jack grabs her and holds his hand to her throat.)* There now. Be very still. *(Macon freezes.)* Hear that? The world's not falling apart. Hear that? *(She nods her head.)* You can handle it, can't you?

MACON. Yes.

JACK. *(He removes his hand from her throat.)* You can handle it just fine. *(He puts his hand on her breast.)* Tell me how you can handle it.

MACON. I can.

JACK. Just fine.

MACON. Yes. *(They embrace with a terrible passion, tearing at each other like beasts. Finally, Macon breaks away. Tears of rage stream down her face.)* Stay away. You viper. You twisted snake. *(Jack looks at her helplessly. He goes to get a drink. Macon straightens her dress and hair, then sits in a chair with her arms folded. Will comes in the door carrying Bess's cape and an arrow. His face is white. He is in a panic.)* Will?

WILL. She's not out there by the pond. She's disappeared.

MACON. That's her cape.

WILL. I found it on the ground. And this. *(Will produces an Indian arrow from under the cape.)*

MACON. Oh my God. Where is she? What's happened?

JACK. Who's is it?

WILL. Looks like Oglala.

JACK. You think Indians got her? *(Macon runs to the door and calls out in the night.)*

MACON. Oh God! Bess! Bess! *(Will grabs Macon in the doorway.)*

WILL. Macon!

MACON. Please, God! Bess! *(Blackout.)*

**End of Act I**

38

## ACT II

### Scene 1

*Five years later. Will's cabin. A spring night.*

*Macon is drinking whiskey. Will and Jack are eating huge pieces of cake. Jack has a mustache.*

JACK. I love this cake.

WILL. It's got a delicate flavor.

MACON. I know it's both your favorite. Happy anniversary, everyone.

WILL. Happy anniversary.

JACK. Happy anniversary.

MACON. Can you believe how fast time travels? Nine years I been living out here on this plain. Youth isn't really all that fleeting like they say. I mean, it seems solid, like it was there, the time you spend being youthful. The rest here, it just flies by, like everything'll be over before you can breathe.

JACK. I don't like to discuss time. It's not my favorite subject, I'd as soon not hear about it.

MACON. I'm sorry, Jack. I know anniversaries are hard for you. Here, let's hand out the presents.

WILL. They're some major presents this year. Some major surprises. *(Macon hands out two gifts that are wrapped identically.)*

MACON. Here you go. I ordered them from the catalogue. I hope you like 'em.

JACK. Thanks.

WILL. Thanks, Macon. *(After opening the gift.)* Well, that's nice. A fancy cup.

MACON. It's a mustache cup. So you won't get your mustache wet when you drink.

JACK. Well, that's a crafty idea. It oughta come in real handy.

WILL. I ain't got no mustache.

MACON. Oh, well, maybe you'll grow one. Jack's looks real nice on him. I think mustaches are the coming thing.

JACK. Here, pour me some cordial. Let me test mine out.

MACON. Alright, let's see.

WILL. Anyway, I could still use it. I'll just drink out of this other side. *(Macon pours Jack a cordial. He drinks from his mustache cup successfully.)*

MACON. Oh, look!

JACK. Pretty handy. Pretty handy.

WILL. Macon, I know there's concern now that the railroad's being rerouted, but I went on and splurged. I got these for you. I know they're what ya wanted. *(Will presents Macon with two red pillows.)* Scarlet plush sofa pillows. Two of 'em.

MACON. Oh, thank you, Will! Thank you! They're so pretty; aren't they pretty!

WILL. They'll cheer up the place.

MACON. They will. Oh, I appreciate it, thank you. Now, if only I could get a new room built, I'd be satisfied. But perhaps not. Seems like I've always something to wish for.

WILL. You do like the pillows though?

MACON. Uh huh.

JACK. I got a gift for you May Ann.

MACON. You do? Why thank you, Jack.

WILL. *(About the gift.)* It looks kinda small. *(Macon opens the gift.)*

MACON. A ring. It's a ring. I cherish rings.

JACK. It's sapphire blue. The color you like best.

MACON. *(Trying the ring on.)* Look, how it fits.

JACK. Just right.

WILL. I don't like him giving you a ring. I'm your husband. You're supposed t'wear my ring.

MACON. Will, I wore that tin band ya gave me till it tore right off.

WILL. I always figured to get ya another one. And now he comes in with this sapphire ring, knowing blue is your favorite color just like you was his wife or something. *(To Jack.)* It's not right! You set your own house on fire, set it aflame, burn

40

it t'ashes and then move in here with us. Just come t'stay and don't ever leave; start giving out rings. Rings are what you give to your wife and she's not your wife. She's my wife. She don't want this ring. Save it for you own damn wife.

MACON. Will, what's wrong with you? You know he ain't got no wife.

WILL. I wouldn't be so sure about that.

MACON. I don't wanna be sure about it. I sure don't wanna be sure. But we've hunted all over for her for years.

JACK. We sent out searching parties.

MACON. We put articles in broadsides; and made inquiries to U.S. Army officers.

JACK. I never wanted to give up hope, but when that hunter from the trading post brought us that scalp ...

MACON. She had such beautiful hair.

JACK. It's all I got left of her. My darling Bess. How I miss her apple butter cheeks now that they're gone.

WILL. People don't always die when they're scalped. You know that, don't ya?

JACK. Yeah.

WILL. Sometimes, they take the scalping knife and cut just a small tuft off at the crown of the head. People recover. It happens a lot. Happy anniversary, Jack. (*Will hands an official looking letter to Jack.*)

JACK. What's this?

WILL. A letter from the U.S. Army. They got your wife. They're gonna deliver her to ya in an Army ambulance. (*Jack grabs the letter. He realizes he can't read it. Macon grabs the letter.*) A Mexican fur trader tipped off a Captain Patch at Fort Sully. The Captain says they had to threaten the Chief, Ottowa, with a massacre 'fore he'd sell her back. They got her for two horses, three blankets, a box of bullets and a sack of glass beads.

MACON. I don't believe this. She's alive.

JACK. I wonder what she'll look like? How do people look when they've been scalped?

MACON. It says here, she's been tattooed on her arms and on her chin.

JACK. Tattooed?

MACON. It don't matter. She won't have changed that much. She's alive. They're bringing her to us and she's still alive.

## End of Scene 1

## Scene 2

*A few days later. Bess stands rooted in the center of the room. She is barefoot. Her skin is dark and burnt; her hair is thin and sun-bleached; her chin has been tattooed. She wears an enormous dress that was lent to her at the fort. Macon and Will stand around her. Jack stands alone gazing at her from the corner of the room.*

MACON. Bess. Bess. Welcome back. Welcome home. We've missed you. We've prayed for your return and here you are back from the vale of death. Fresh from pandemonium.

WILL. I don't think she likes being inside. I bet, you ain't used to having a roof over your head? It agitates ya, don't it?

JACK. No point in pumping her. She don't wanna talk.

MACON. Well, I'm sure it was an awful experience but it's over. Right now you probably could use a bath. Will, go bring a couple of buckets of water for me from the well. Jack, you go fetch the washtub.

JACK. Alright, but I bet she don't remember what a bath is. *(Will and Jack exit.)*

MACON. Everything's gonna be fine. Just fine. Just very fine. In honor of your homecoming we're having a big juicy ham. *(Bess retches.)* What's wrong?

BESS. Thought of hog eaters make me choke.

MACON. What's wrong with hog? It's just pig. It's just pork.

BESS. *(Fiercely.)* Mud and water animal, bad.

MACON. Well, we could have something else. Vegetables. A lot of vegetables and pumpkin pie for dessert. You remember our pumpkin patch? Well, anyway, it's doing real well. People come by at Halloween time and pick out their own jackerlanterns. We make a little money from that venture. It comes in handy. It's not like times are flush around here. Wheat prices have dropped and the railroad's been rerouted. We're in bad debt 'cause of purchasing three fields we don't have the resources to work. But like they say, trouble comes in twos. I'm hoping someday things'll be different and we'll have an abundance. Don't you remember me at all? I'm your friend. I taught you how to whistle. *(Macon whistles.)* Don't ya remember? *(Macon whistles again; she stops. Bess looks at her. Macon whistles with a desperate intent. Bess whistles back to her, very softly.)* Bess.

BESS. Friend.

MACON. Right. yes. It's gonna be alright. Everything'll be just like it was. Sour milk will help bleach down that dark skin, and we'll get ya a brand-new dress. A blue one.

BESS. Blue.

MACON. Yeah, one that'll fit ya just right. Lord, that captain's wife musta been bigger than a mule. A real mud and water animal, that captain's wife.

BESS. Oh, big. *(They laugh.)*

MACON. I don't know but somehow, you survived it.

BESS. I picture you.

MACON. What? You pictured me?

BESS. Hunt the elephant.

MACON. The elephant?

BESS. Bang, bang, bang.

MACON. Oh, Bess. I think you're gonna need some false curls. And maybe some cornstarch over that chin. Or veils. Sweet little net veils. *(Bess feels her chin.)*

BESS. Ottawa.

MACON. What?

BESS. To be his bride. They mark me.

MACON. You were a bride?

BESS. *(She nods.)* Two ... two children. Chante, Hunke-she. Ottawa. I thought he was true one. He gave me black horse.

MACON. No, no. He was bad. He was an Indian. He was bad.

BESS. Yes, bad. Sold me. Sold me cheap. Two horses, blanket, beads, bullets. Cheap.

MACON. Bess, you can't — don't ever tell Jack.

BESS. No.

MACON. No one else. Don't tell anyone else. *(Jack enters with the washtub.)* Jack. Jack, she's talking. She don't like pork, but she's talking.

BESS. Jack.

JACK. Look at her. She's disgusting.

MACON. Jack, don't —

JACK. *(Running on.)* She smells like old cheese.

MACON. Stop it!

JACK. *(Running on.)* I wish they'd never found her.

MACON. Hush up! Hush! *(Jack grabs Macon passionately in his arms, smelling and caressing her. He rams his fingers through her hair, tearing out her combs.)*

JACK. I want you. Not her. Only you. Understand me?

MACON. *(Overlapping.)* Let me go. Let go. Get away. *(Macon pushes him away.)*

JACK. She may be back. But nothing's changed. *(Jack exits. Macon turns to Bess who stares at her with anguished eyes.)*

MACON. Bess, please, he — I'm sorry. I never — You must believe me. I thought you were dead. They brought us your scalp. You were gone so long. So many years.

BESS. No. You. I saw. *(Pointing to Macon's combs.)* Combs. You gave him. He held them. I saw.

MACON. It'll be over now. I promise. I'll make it up to you. I'll make it right, I swear. Everything will be just the same.

### End of Scene 2

### Scene 3

*A week later. A hot summer night.*

*Will sits outside the barn hammering together a chain. He now has a moustache.*

*Macon enters.*

MACON. Have you finished?

WILL. Not yet.

MACON. It's always hot. Summer's almost over and it hasn't rained once. There's no relief.

WILL. I think you're working the ox too hard. It needs more rest. More water.

MACON. We have to work the fields.

WILL. If the ox gets sick, it'll be over for us.

MACON. What do you want? The bank is breathing down our necks. When will you finish that?

WILL. I don't know.

MACON. I need it by morning. I can't chase her and be in the fields. Not in this heat.

WILL. I don't like the idea of this.

MACON. I don't know how else to stop her from running away. She bites through rope.

WILL. Why not let her go?

MACON. She's my friend, I have to save her. We got to be patient. We got to wean her from her savage ways. She'll come around in time. God, you look —

WILL. What?

MACON. I don't know, old, I guess.

WILL. Maybe it's the moustache.

MACON. Oh yeah. You have a — You grew one. *(Macon exits. Will continues hammering on the chain.)*

### End of Scene 3


### Scene 4


*A month later. A hot day.*

*Outside Will's cabin. Jack aims his six-shooter at an offstage target. He fires the gun. He misses his target.*

JACK. Damn. *(Jacks shoots two more bullets. He keeps missing his offstage target. This puts him in a rage.)* Damn, hell, damn. *(Ma-*

*con appears from the direction of the barn.)*

MACON.  What are ya shooting at?

JACK.  Playing cards. I used t'could split 'em at thirty paces.

MACON.  Stop wasting powder. *(Jack turns around and points the gun at her.)* You don't scare me anymore.

JACK.  And you don't make me smile. *(Jack lowers his gun.)*

MACON.  Your wife's here for that.

JACK.  Uh huh.

MACON.  *(Softly, intensely.)* It's all over between us.

JACK.  It wasn't over in the barn last night.

MACON.  Well, now it is.

JACK.  You been telling me that for some time. I'm starting to doubt your word.

MACON.  Go clean out the chicken coop. Earn your keep.

JACK.  I still smell you. *(Jack embraces Macon. She responds.)*

MACON.  *(With loathing.)* I wanna be rid of you. Why can't I be rid of you? *(Bess appears. She wears a blue dress and is barefoot. She has a shackle around her foot and is chained to an offstage stake. Macon and Jack break apart. They stare at her for a brief moment before Jack exits toward the barn.)* Where're your shoes? You have to wear shoes. We all wear shoes around here. And you need to keep that veil on to cover your face. Those tattoos are not proper. People frown on 'em. *(Will enters. He looks very glum.)* Will! Will, you're back. How'd it go? Not good? Not so good? What? Huh? Speak! Will you speak!

WILL.  They won't renew the note. They're repossessing the steeltipped plow and the barbwire. They want our horse and mule and hogs, even our ox. Everything we used as security.

MACON.  They can't take our livelihood. The last two years, there's been a drought.

WILL.  They've heard all about the drought.

MACON.  I'll go into town. I'll fix this myself. You can never get anything done. You're incapable. I'll get my hat and gloves. I'll get this settled. *(Macon goes into the cabin.)*

WILL.  *(To Bess.)* I understand why you wanna run away. I'd let you go, but she keeps the key. Me, I'm not sure why I stay. I don't know what I expect to get. She used to be nice to me sometimes for very short intervals of time. Not anymore. I

46

don't know what I expect to get now. I mean, from now on. *(Macon appears from the cabin wearing a hat and gloves. She carries Bess's shoes and veil.)*

MACON. Have you hitched the wagon?

WILL. Not yet.

MACON. Go do it. *(Will exits for the barn. Throughout the following, Macon dresses Bess in the shoes and veil.)* Will Curtis is a very commonplace type man. Really, anyone who would spend money to buy a glass eye makes me laugh. You'll see, I'll go into that bank and come out with a loan for a windmill, a gang plow and twenty cord of barbwire. Great invention, barbwire. Keeps what you want in and all the rest of it out. There, that's better. That blue dress looks good. You look pretty in it. I sacrificed a lot to get it for you. I want to make you happy. I'd take these chains off, if only you would stay. Will you stay? Bess. Bess. *(A beat.)* I wish you'd speak to me. *(A beat.)* No. Alright. I'll bring some daisies back for you, if I see them on the road. *(Macon exits. Bess jerks violently at her chain. She struggles with fierce rage pounding the chain. She moans with unbearable despair and finally sinks to the ground exhausted. Jack and Professor Elmore Crome, a distinguished looking young man, enter from the barn road. Jack holds money in his hand.)*

JACK. *(Indicating Bess.)* Here she is. Right there. Go ahead. Look at her. *(Jack removes her veiled hat.)*

ELMORE. Why is she chained up?

JACK. We've had to restrain her to prevent her from returning to the wilds.

ELMORE. I see. Mrs. Flan?

JACK. I didn't say you could talk to her. *(Elmore hands Jack another bill.)* Alright. But she don't talk back.

ELMORE. How do you do, Mrs. Flan. I'm Professor Elmore Crome. It's an honor to make your acquaintance. I read about your brutal capture in a broadside. What an amazing feat to have survived such an ordeal. You're a remarkable woman. I'm in awe of your strength and courage.

JACK. She don't understand nothing you say.

ELMORE. One more word, please. I just — I just wish so much I could hear about your experiences from your own lips.

47

I was hoping we could write a book together. A book that would help prevent others from falling prey to similar atrocities.

JACK.   Write a book. Why she ain't spoke one word since they brought her back. *(Sympathetically.)* She's just a pitiful specimen.

ELMORE.   Please, I have a gift for you. I brought a gift. *(He hands her a silver mirror wrapped in a handkerchief. She looks at herself in the mirror. She touches the tattoos on her chin.)* I know people would want to read about you. People all over the world. I'm sure you have so much to tell. So many adventures to impart. You must know a great deal about Indian ways. About their lives; about their treachery.

JACK.   That's enough now. *(Bess looks Elmore in the eye. He looks back at her.)* I said time to go.

ELMORE.   Good afternoon, Mrs. Flan. In all honesty, I must say, you have the bravest eyes I have ever witnessed. *(Jack and Elmore start to leave.)*

BESS.   Don't —

ELMORE.   *(Stopping.)* What?

BESS.   Go.

ELMORE.   Yes.

BESS.   I do. I know treachery. I could write book. A big book. All about treachery.

ELMORE.   Excellent.

### End of Scene 4

### Scene 5

*Two months later.*

*The yard in front of Will's cabin. Will rushes onstage. He is breathing hard. His eyes are grief-stricken. He stops, sits down and puts his hands over his face.*

*Jack appears from the cabin carrying a pitcher of cool punch and two tin cups.*

48

JACK. 'Morning, Will. How're things going?

WILL. The wheat's burnt dead. There's no saving it. The ox just collapsed down in the dirt. He's alive, he's struggling but he can't get back up. Could I have a drink? I'm parched.

JACK. I made this beverage for the Professor and Bess. They get real thirsty working on the book.

WILL. I just want a sip.

JACK. Sorry. (*Macon appears from the fields. She hauls a load of wilted corn. She is in a state of mad frenzy.*)

MACON. Christ. Will. The ox. The look in his eyes. God, how he's suffering. Did you get the gun?

WILL. Not yet.

MACON. Go get it. Shoot him! Kill him! Blow out his brains! I can't bear it! He keeps looking at me like I owe him something!!! (*Will goes into the cabin to get a gun.*) Where were you last night?

JACK. I didn't come.

MACON. I waited for you.

JACK. I couldn't get away.

MACON. Why not? (*Bess is heard singing "Down In The Valley."*)

JACK. Because of her.

MACON. Her.

JACK. Yeah.

MACON. Did you stay with her?

JACK. What could I do? She's my wife. (*Bess and Elmore enter. Bess carries a parasol. She wears a cape and new shoes. She doesn't wear her veil. We see her tattoos. Elmore has a pad and pen. He is constantly taking notes.*)

ELMORE. What a voice you have! Like an angel!

BESS. Every time the Oglalas raised scalps on a pole and threatened to slay me, I'd sing for them. They'd fall to their knees and listen to my song, entranced, like charmed wolves. Ottawa, the head man, gave me strings of beads; others gave me acorns, seeds, ground nuts, feathers. Any treasure they possessed so I would favor them with my singing.

ELMORE. Amazing. Quite a provocative tale. Ah! The punch! Please serve Mrs. Flan a glass. I'm sure she must be parched.

*(Jack serves punch, then holds Bess's parasol to shade her.)*
BESS. Oh, no. Why I often went months without a drop of any drink during my stay in captivity.
ELMORE. Fascinating. How did you survive?
BESS. I'd chew constantly on a small stick to help prevent parching, or I'd hunt for wild fruits that grow all in abundance. *(Bess whistles softy.)*
ELMORE. You are an amazing creation. How anyone could have endured such hardship.
MACON. She pictured me.
ELMORE. What?
MACON. She pictured me. *(Will comes out of the cabin with a gun.)*
WILL. Macon, I have the gun.
MACON. Not now.
WILL. I — I'm going to shoot the ox. It has to be done. He's suffering. *(Will heads toward the field.)* Won't you please come?
MACON. Shoot it by yourself.
WILL. I'll need somebody to help me slaughter it. Jack, would you?
JACK. The Professor pays you for our room and board. I'm no hired hand. *(Will exits.)*
MACON. Bess, tell the Professor how you pictured me when you was captured.
BESS. I thought about ya. I thought about all my loved ones back home.
ELMORE. It must have been unbearable — your sorrow.
BESS. It's true, I've suffered. But I come out here drunk with western fever. I wanted to see the elephant. To hunt down the elephant. Bang! Bang! Bang! I savor the boundlessness of it all! The wild flavor!
ELMORE. You take my breath away. How powerfully you speak in your simple, unadorned language. When your book comes out we must send you on the lyceum lecture circuit. What a sensation you'd make.
BESS. You flatter me, really.
MACON. My Lord, yes. Just imagine Bess on a big stage in front of a whole room full of people. Such a shy little thing.

She'd die of fright. You need somebody who's got a real knack for that sort of thing. Ya know, I once played the Virgin Mary in a Christmas pageant. I had such a saintly face, an unearthly glow. I cried real tears when the Innkeeper told us there was no room for us at his inn.

ELMORE. *(A beat.)* It seems to me, the sun's very bright here. Why don't we go work in the willow grove down by the pond.

BESS. Yes. I'll tell you all about how the horrid hell hounds tattooed my face with sharp sticks dipped in weed juices and the powder from blue mud stones.

ELMORE. Monstrous savages. Godless perpetrators of butchery. *(Elmore and Bess exit.)*

MACON. I wore a blue robe as the Virgin Mary. Blue looks good on me. It's my best color, although I did not know it at the time.

JACK. Something about you's changed. You've lost the stars in your shoes. You used to run everywhere you'd go.

MACON. Well, what about you? Look at you. Serving punch, toting parasols, bowing and scraping.

JACK. I do, what I do.

MACON. You live like a leech.

JACK. Would you give me back the ring I gave you? I want to give it to my wife. *(An offstage gunshot is heard.)*

MACON. Take it. Here, take it.

WILL. *(Offstage.)* God, it's still alive. Macon!

MACON. Good, it's over. Good.

WILL. *(Offstage.)* It's looking at me.

MACON. I'll kill it. I'll blow it dead. I'll do it! *(Macon exits. Jack looks after her. He tosses the ring up in the air and starts offstage. As he goes toward Bess and the Professor, we hear one last shot.)*

**End of Scene 5**

## Scene 6

*The following spring.*

*Will sits alone in the yard. Bess and Elmore are gathered in Will's cabin. Elmore is looking through a portfolio taking out letters, contracts, illustrations, etc. Bess is waving a check through the air.*

ELMORE.  A phenomenon. Your book is a phenomenon!

BESS.  I've hit pay dirt!

ELMORE.  *(Looking at a sheet of figures.)* It's astonishing! No one can believe it!

BESS.  I must have a pet song bird! We'll sing a duet together!

ELMORE.  Over sixty thousand copies sold!

BESS.  Oh, and get me a giant harp with gold cherubs and an ice palace to keep it in.

ELMORE.  Whatever your heart desires.

BESS.  *(Singing.)* Roses are blue, oh, roses are blue ...

ELMORE.  *(Overlapping.)* Now I have some correspondence that requires your attention.

BESS.  Yes, yes, proceed; proceed.

ELMORE.  *(Presenting a letter.)* The President of Indian Affairs wants to dine with you at the White House the day you arrive in Washington.

BESS.  Oh, delightful. I'm delighted. How thrilling! I hope they don't serve any pig.

ELMORE.  No, of course not. I'll alert them to your wishes. All pig shall be banned. Now here's an inquiry from actor-manager-playwright Dion Boucicault. He wants to adapt your book into a hit play.

BESS.  Dion Boucicault? Who's that?

ELMORE.  He's very famous.

BESS.  Oh, alright then, I consent. *(Jack enters carrying some luggage. He has shaved his moustache.)*

ELMORE.  *(Handing her an illustration.)* Now here's the portrait of you that we want to include in the second edition.

BESS. Oh, dear.

ELMORE. I find it very sensitive, yet I feel there's a deep sense of inner strength.

BESS. Hmm. My eyes are too close together. I've got beautiful hair, but my eyes are too close together. *(To Jack.)* Don't you agree?

JACK. No.

BESS. But they're closer together than an average person's eyes, wouldn't you say?

JACK. I don't know. No.

BESS. Well, how close together do you think an average person's eyes are?

JACK. I don't know.

BESS. Then stop offering opinions on subjects you're completely stupid on.

JACK. Alright.

BESS. Don't be so agreeable. Finish fetching our bags and move them out to the carriage. We don't want to miss our train. *(Jack exits into another room.)* Do we really have to bother with him?

ELMORE. Of course, it's entirely your decision, but I'm afraid an anguished, adoring husband makes for excellent pathos.

BESS. Yes. Well, then. I'll manage.

ELMORE. Good. Excellent. Now, according to this schedule, you'll be doing up to one hundred and fifty lectures this season. You stand to profit over twenty-five thousand dollars from the lecture circuit alone.

BESS. Angels sing, devils dance.

ELMORE. Mr. William Sutton is the promoter for the tour. He's a very successful land speculator who is deeply devoted to western expansion and the concept of manifest destiny. He'd like for you to sign this contract agreeing to expound certain philosophical beliefs from the podium.

BESS. Philosophical beliefs? I'm not sure I got any of them. Here, let me see the paper. *(Bess takes the contract and reads it thoroughly. Macon enters the area in front of the cabin. She spots Will.)*

MACON. Repossession. Repossession. That one word they

clung to like a pack of sick dogs. They're taking our home. There's nothing to be done, unless they get fifty dollars. Fifty dollars. I asked the man with the red beard if he'd accept potatoes as partial payment. He laughed at me like I was a brand-new joke.

WILL. I told you how it come out. Things are finished here. We'll have to go somewhere else. Start fresh.

MACON. I'd rather choke to death right here in the sun. *(Inside the cabin Jack enters with the bags. He starts for the cabin door. Bess stops him.)*

BESS. Jack, don't forget that basket there, I packed us some food for the road.

JACK. Great. What is it?

BESS. Cornbread. *(Jack nods, picks up the basket and leaves the cabin. He goes into the yard. Macon spots him.)*

MACON. Jack, where're you going?

JACK. The Professor's come for us. Bess's book's selling like wildfire. We're going on a lecture circuit. We've become important people.

MACON. You're leaving right now?

JACK. That's right.

MACON. How long will you be gone?

JACK. For good, I hope.

MACON. God. How will I ever stand living in this great wasteland all alone.

JACK. *(Indicating Will.)* Ya still got him.

MACON. Yeah. Listen, Jack, I'm in trouble. I need fifty dollars to save the homestead.

JACK. I ain't got no money.

MACON. Well, would you talk to Bess for me? Would you put in a good word?

JACK. You talk to her. She's your friend.

MACON. That's right. You're right. She's my friend. I done a lot for her. A whole lot. Goodbye, Jack.

JACK. So long, May Ann.

MACON. I'll always remember you as the possessor of a very handsome pair of eyes. *(Jack exits. Will stares ahead, trying to decide why he doesn't care about killing these people. Macon goes into the cabin. Will exits.)* Bess. I need to talk to you. It's concerning a personal situation. Good afternoon, Professor.

ELMORE. Yes, well ... good afternoon, Mrs. Curtis. *(Elmore gets up and goes into the yard.)*

MACON. I heard you're leaving. You're off. You've made it in the big time.

BESS. That's how it appears.

MACON. I don't begrudge you. I saw it coming. People lap up them atrocity stories. They read 'em all the time in them penny dreadfuls. Now you go and give 'em the real factualized version. Ya even got the marks t'prove it. People'll get up outta their homes and come down to them big halls to see them marks. Them tattoos. People thrive on seeing freaks.

BESS. Well, I'm glad you don't begrudge me.

MACON. No. Why would I?

BESS. No reason. I just thought you wanted to write a book, a novel. You spoke about it. But I guess that was more like a pipe dream, a childish fantasy. Nothing to be taken seriously.

MACON. I had a book in mind at one point. I was gonna write about my adventures.

BESS. I guess, you just never had any, did ya?

MACON. I had some. Some things happened to me.

BESS. Not that much, though.

MACON. Well, I never got my face scarred.

BESS. Do you wish you had?

MACON. Why would I?

BESS. Because, maybe you would like to be ... remarkable. But you're not. You look forward to things by decades. You're settled, staid and dreamless. I see it haunts you how ya just can't compare t'me. To Bess Johnson, the woman who survived five adventurous years of Indian captivity. Who returned to write the book of the century and be adored by throngs all over the globe.

MACON. You don't fool me. I know how ya done it all. You pictured me. You stole from me. You stole me. I showed you how to walk and speak and fight and dream. I should have written that book. People should be clamoring t'meet me; t'talk t'me. I'm the real thing; you're just a watered down milktoast version. Them Indians stole the wrong woman.

BESS. Is that a fact?

MACON. Yeah, it is.

BESS. Well, maybe it ain't too late. Maybe you've got one more chance. Here, take this knife. Take this ink. Go ahead. Cut open your face. Pour in the ink. Go be me, if you think you can. If you think you're so brave. I'll let you be me. You can do my tour. People will rise to their feet and clamor for you. Go ahead. The Oglalas rejoice in wounding themselves. They do it for prayer. They do it to celebrate grief. Come on, do it, celebrate, rejoice, do it — all it is is your face.

MACON. Bess, please — I always cared for you. I always did.

BESS. Then do it. Cut it. To shreds; all to shreds.

MACON. I did, you know. I always did.

BESS. Then do it. Cut it; do it. *(Macon takes the knife. Holds it to her face, then sets it down.)*

MACON. I'm not gonna cut myself up. I don't wanna be scarred for life.

BESS. *(A beat.)* No. That would cost too much. And you've gotten so measly you watch every egg, nickel, and biscuit. *(Bess starts putting on her hat and gloves.)*

MACON. I know we don't like each other. We used to be friends. But somehow we drifted apart. Still you have to admit, you have to see, that you owe me something.

BESS. What do I owe you?

MACON. You — well, you owe me — fifty dollars. At least, fifty dollars. I gave you shoes when you had none and food and coffee and clothes and lodging. I even brought you blue ribbons and a blue dress. Whatever your heart desired, I gave to you.

BESS. Maybe it never occurred t'you. Maybe you never realized the fact, but people don't like being beholding. They resent always needing and always owing. And pretty soon they come to resent whoever it is they been taking from.

MACON. I do. I know that. You've resented me all along.

BESS. Yeah, I believe I have and I don't want you resenting me. So why don't we just call it even.

MACON. But I gotta have it. The fifty dollars. I need it to

56

save my homestead. They're gonna throw me out on the dusty road. You can't do this to me.

BESS. Honey, I'd rip the wings off an angel if I thought they'd help me fly. *(Bess leaves the cabin and goes out into the yard. Macon follows her.)*

MACON. You owe me! I'm due! You can't deny me what's mine! I gave you green biscuits; I combed your hair; I taught you to whistle!

ELMORE. Are you ready?

BESS. Yeah.

ELMORE. Did you read the contract?

BESS. They want me to demand the immediate extermination of all Indian tribes.

ELMORE. That's correct.

BESS. I got no problem with that. Just make sure wherever we go I have a basket of golden tulips to greet me. They're my favorite flower, tulips. *(Bess and Elmore exit as Macon screams after them.)*

MACON. You thief! Robber — thief! Tulips are mine! They belong to me! I seen the picture! You never did! *(Will enters wearing his eye patch and carrying a satchel.)* God, Will. God. She wouldn't give me the money. She wouldn't give me nothing. She owes me, too. She knows she does. I was her friend. God, I'd like to kill her. I'd like to tear off her head and feed her brains to rabid rats. The selfish, back-biting, stuck-up, black-hearted Indian whore!

WILL. Macon, I'm leaving here. I'm heading west.

MACON. West? Where west?

WILL. Don't know.

MACON. Maybe we'll try Idaho. They got that Turkey red wheat in Idaho. It's a hard-kernelded wheat. You can grow it all spring.

WILL. I don't want you with me.

MACON. What?

WILL. My first wife, Barbara Jane, well, I loved her. And I remember she loved me. But you never loved me and I never loved you. That's all it's been. I don't want it no more.

MACON. You leaving me here? With nothing?

WILL. This is yours. Catch. (*Will throws her his glass eye. She catches it.*) I bought it for you. It never done me no good. (*Will exits. Macon paces around the yard tossing the glass eye back and forth, from hand to hand.*)
MACON. I got nothing. Nothing. After all this time. (*A beat.*) Nothing.

## End of Scene 6

## Scene 7

*Fifteen years later.*

*A hotel suite in St. Louis. Bess drinks a glass of whiskey. Elmore holds a copy of the St. Louis* Chronicle.

ELMORE. Are you sure you want to hear this?
BESS. Uh huh.
ELMORE. It's not very good.
BESS. That seems to be the trend.
ELMORE. It's appallingly written.
BESS. Go ahead, Elmore, it's the last one I'll ever get.
ELMORE. The St. Louis *Chronicle* says, "Mrs. Bess Johnson delivered her speech with impassioned fervor. However, the story seemed excessive and outdated like a worn-out melodrama one would read in a dime novel. The text lacked all orderly progressions and seemed to ramble and roam incoherently, as though perhaps Mrs. Johnson had had a drop too many."
BESS. A drop too many! They can't actually expect me to deliver those speeches sans intoxication. What a tight-lipped powder puff. What a worm-ridden toad.
ELMORE. (*Folding up the paper.*) Yes, well, let's put it away.
BESS. God. I can't tell you what a relief it will be to never again to have to rhapsodize about writing with fish blood and being scantily-clad in a thin bark skirt.
ELMORE. Yes. I'm well aware we have played ourselves out. People are no longer interested in hearing about the untamed

savages. Times have changed. Indians today are beloved circus performers. Yesterday, I read in a broadside that they finally arrested your old friend, Ottowa, down by the Pecos River. They'd been hunting him for years. He was the last holdout. The lone one.

BESS. Ottowa, I didn't know he was still alive.

ELMORE. He's not. He drank a lantern of kerosene the night they captured him.

BESS. Oh.

ELMORE. *(Presenting her with contracts.)* Well, here are the final papers disbanding our long and lucrative union. They're all in order. You'll find everything's as we discussed.

BESS. I'm sure they are. I'll just have my attorneys read it over before I sign it.

ELMORE. I admire your consistency, Bess. All these years and you've never trusted me once.

BESS. Sorry, Elmore. I tried that. It never really worked out for me, *(Jack enters smoking a large black cigar. He is dressed dapperly.)*

JACK. 'Afternoon.

ELMORE. Hello, Jack.

BESS. What's that awful thing?

JACK. A ten cent cigar. I won it betting on the comic mule races down at the tent show.

ELMORE. Ah, yes, how was the tent show?

JACK. Pathetic, small town dredge. The freaks were even third rate: armless boy; electric girl; skeleton dude. Oh, but you'll never guess who I ran into. What's her name? We used to know her back when. Her husband wore an eye patch.

BESS. Macon?

JACK. Yes, I think that was it.

BESS. Macon Hill.

JACK. You should see her. Disgusting. She's got some syphilitic disease. It's broken out all over her face. She was working at a little booth dispensing whiskey and tobacco and raisins. I bought some raisins from her. She didn't recognize me. I had to laugh when I saw she had newspaper stuck in her clothes to stay warm. I remember her always thinking she had it so good.

BESS. Your cigar is foul. Put it out. Get it out. *(Jack puts out the cigar.)* God, you're an imbecile. Coming in here, filling the room with your vile smoke. You've given me a sick head. I'm going out for some air. Clear out this room before I get back. *(Bess exits.)*

JACK. Christ, why am I ever nice to that woman? You're lucky you're getting out from under her. I'm stuck with her for life. Tomorrow we leave for our White Plains estate. We'll retire there together till the end of our days. What will it be like?

ELMORE. She can be difficult. But I think, underneath it all, she has real affection for you.

JACK. You think she does?

ELMORE. It's the sort of thing that's only apparent to an outsider.

JACK. Well, I'll say one thing, she'll never find anyone who'll treat her better than I do. She oughta know that by now. I'm her one true one.

### End of Scene 7

### Scene 8

*A few hours later. Early evening.*

*Macon's tent. Macon sits alone in the dimly lit tent drinking and playing solitaire. There are sores on her face.*

BESS. *(Offstage.)* Hello? Anybody here?
MACON. Yeah. *(Bess enters.)*
BESS. Macon?
MACON. Bess?
BESS. I heard you were here.
MACON. Jack tell you?
BESS. Yeah.
MACON. I seen him this afternoon. He bought some raisins.

He wouldn't speak to me though.

BESS. Well, you know him.

MACON. Yeah. Why'd you come?

BESS. I — don't know. I was — remembering ...

MACON. Uh huh.

BESS. So much.

MACON. Well.

BESS. How you been?

MACON. Great. Just great. Yeah, for a time I was raking in the green selling this Indian Remedy. A cure for your opium, morphine, liquor and tobacco habit. Hell of a cure it was, too. Then I got this stuff coming out on my face and people kinda eased off on purchasing the cure. But for a time there, I was flush. How 'bout you?

BESS. I don't know. Maybe other people's lives have made more sense than mine.

MACON. It's always a possibility.

BESS. Oh, well. There it is, I guess.

MACON. Yeah, laid right out behind you like a lizard's tail.

BESS. Today I — Well, today I heard that Ottowa, the head man — my husband, was captured. He, ah, poisoned himself on a lantern of kerosene. I don't know why, but it's hard. I'd always thought I might — but now I won't — ever see him once more.

MACON. It's a shame how things turn out. I swear to God, I wish I knew how it could be different.

BESS. Uh huh. Me too.

MACON. 'Least ya got out there and saw the elephant.

BESS. Yeah. Yeah, the Oglalas knew such beautiful places. I saw rivers that were so clear you could see every pebble and fish. And the water was any color you could dream: pink and turquoise; gold and white; lime green.

MACON. Hell of a time you had with the Oglalas.

BESS. Beautiful time I had. Hey, you ever hear from Will Curtis?

MACON. Nah. Will got caught in a threshing machine back in '87. Got his leg cut off in the blade. Bled t'death in a field. Funny, I always figured he'd go piecemeal.

61

BESS. Yeah.

MACON. You know, when I was younger, I never knew who I was, what I wanted, where I was going or how to get there. Now that I'm older, I don't know none of that either.

BESS. Well, one thing I wanted, one thing I know I wanted was, well, I don't know, I guess you'd call it true love. And when I got them three letters from that man, that man, Michael Flan, who wrote to me about the size of the sky, I thought it was all right there, all within my grasp and all I had t'do was come out west and there it'd be.

MACON. Thought you'd just reach up and touch it like a star.

BESS. Yeah. Thought I might. *(Bess reaches her hand up as if she were grabbing a star.)* Aah!

MACON. Feel a chill?

BESS. Just a small one.

MACON. Bess?

BESS. Huh.

MACON. I, well, I've had a bad pain in my heart all day today. I'm scared and it troubles me, but I expect I'll die soon.

BESS. ... What can I do?

MACON. Nothing t'do. I just wanted somebody t'tell, that's all. Someone to tell.

BESS. Well, you can tell me.

MACON. There ain't much t'tell.

BESS. Maybe not, but I'm glad you looked my way.

MACON. Uh huh. Well. Yeah.

BESS. Hey, do you still whistle?

MACON. Me? I — God — I — *(Then definitely.)* No. *(A long beat, then Macon whistles a tune, Bess whistles back. The women both laugh from deep in the bottom of their hearts. The lights fade to blackout.)*

## END OF PLAY

# SCENERY / FURNITURE / PROPS

## ACT I

### Scene 1

Onstage ranche bench — fastened to deck with stage screws

Onstage wanted poster

Macon — satchel, knife in boot, platter with green biscuits, pad and pencil in pocket

Will — eyepatch

Jack — gunbelt with unloaded pistol

Bess — suitcase with 3 letters in interior pocket (tied with tan ribbon)

### Scene 2

On wall — rifle in rack, two rabbit skins, antlers above door, traps and chains under shelf

On shelf — cigar box, broken lantern, tobacco tin, tin cup, round tin, bottle, fry pan, hammer, glass jar with "beef jerky" (strips of raspberry fruit leather), water jar with lid, lantern (circuited)

On shelf corner — canvas bucket

Jack's table and chair

On table — sieve and chamois cloth (for polishing pistol)

Iron stove with dirty iron pot

Axe leaning against wall, held by wired hook

Mattress on floor, covered with quilt, blanket, afghan, trousers, beaver skin, badger skin, wool blanket, shirts, flour sack, rags, 2 scarves

### Scene 3

Worktable — wooden bowl with wooden spoon, pots and pans, dish basin

Will's table (C.) — working tools (knives, axe, chains)

Next to table — barrel with 2 picks

1 chair R. of table

Will's bed (set up L.) — pillow, quilt, ruby ring wrapped
in pillow in handerchief, jacket
Mantelpiece — small photograph on wall above mantel.
Will's tin mirror, daguerrotype of Barbara Jane in frame,
kerosene lantern (circuited), wide ceramic mug, fireplace poker (hanging by fireplace)
1 chair pulled up to mantelpiece, draped with Will's shirt
Coat pegs by door — harness and horsecollar
Will's long rifle

## Scene 4
Tree (branch swung onstage from D.L.)

## Scene 5
Jack's pistol (loaded with 3 cardridges) — in holster
Jack's mining equipment — lantern, rope in coil, pick
Macon's bundle — shoes and coffee tied up in cloth

## Scene 6
Macon's walking stick
Macon's field glasses (on leather strap — around her
neck)
Two rough-cut logs for Will and Jack combat

## Scene 7
Setting same as Act I, Scene 2, except:
Quilt hung over door, afghan hung under shelf, wool
blanket on wall next to table, trousers and beaver
skin on wall next to door, badger skin beneath
afghan, rags/scarves/shirts stuffed in corners
Deerskin on Jack's table (for Jack to wrap up in)
STRIKE sieve, pot from stove, jerky jar
ADD bowl to shelf, torn mattress with straw and corn
kernels on floor, crate U.L. with hidden baby clothes
and small cloth sack of corn meal (masa harina),
grey tin plate on mattress with a few wheat kernels

## Scene 8

Setting same as Act I, Scene 3, except:

ADD to worktable — cordial bottle with cork, clean rag

ADD to Will's table — white tablecloth, 2 whiskey
glasses (partially filled)

SHIFT both chairs to table, barrel to under coat pegs

ADD to coat pegs — Will's bearskin coat, Will's bearskin
hat, dressing cape, dressing jacket

ADD to mantelpiece — copper kettle (with warm water)
hung over electric fire, Christmas greenery, Will's
mirror, Macon's hairbrush, oil lamp (circuited), painting above mantel

ADD to bed — extra brown blanket (to wrap Bess),
glass eye in box with homemade card (under pillow)

ADD bar to door

ADD curtains to window

## Scene 9

2 joined fence pieces

Jack's tin cake plate with 1 large piece of poundcake,
napkin

Will — 2 pressed shirts

## Scenes 10 and 11

Setting same as Act 1, Scene 8, except:

Will's long rifle on hooks over door

Will's original bed by wall — with new blanket and
cover, copper box of long cartridges under bed

Jack's new bed (D.R.) — with Jack's socks

On coat pegs — dressing cape, dressing hat, dressing
shirt, dressing jacket; Macon's cape for Bess

Barrel under coat pegs (ADD bar from door in centre
slot)

Mantelpiece — mantel lace, 2 books, glass jar with silk
daisies

Worktable — mason jar with water, 4 tin mugs, stack of
4 tin plates/knives/forks/napkins, Will's whittling and
Barlow knife, cake plate with single piece of pound-

cake, coffee pot, 2 whiskey glasses, tin of saddle soap, polishing rag, Jack's boots, (batter bowl comes down from shelf, turned to show batter drips)

Will's table — new tablecloth, Macon's mirror, box with 2 hair combs and blue ribbon, Macon's hairbrush

4 chairs around table


## ACT II

### Scene 1

2 beds removed during intermission shift, table moved to under window; change painting above mantel

Worktable — jar with pickles, box of Betsy Ross tea, cordial bottle, washbasin, hidden: 2 moustache cups wrapped in cloth, tied with ribbon

Will's table — new tablecloth, large bowl, 2 red satin sofa pillows covered with brown cloth (under table), cow painting above table on wall, two chairs at table

Mantelpiece — Macon's hairbrush, mirror, china piece, clock, additional book, haircomb box (from Act I, Scenes 10 and 11)

Sofa (set turntable center)

Side table — 3 filled cordial glasses, 3 small china cake plates with cake remnants, 3 small cloth napkins

Coat pegs — dressing cape, Jack's gunbelt with loaded pistol (3 cardridges) and Jack's hat

Rocking chair

Personals — Will's U.S. Army letter, Jack's sapphire ring in handerkchief twist, Macon's combs (check no tin band top of act)

N.B.: On turntable right — two wagon wheels, shovel, hoe, crate, pieces of yoke, ganged together, leaning against wall

Will's long rifle restored over door; door bar struck

**Scene 2**
    Same as Act II, Scene 1
    Jack's washtub (carried from L.)

**Scene 3**
    Small bench
    Wooden chair (next to bench)
    Macon's lantern (battery flame)
    Will's anvil — reinforced crate with iron plate
    Will's wooden tool box with rags, hammer, dressing tools
    On anvil — long chain, blacksmith's pliers and sledge
        hammer
    Will's lantern (battery flame)
    Harrow
    Rusty trap hanging on wall (hides cable from Jack's
        uncircuited lantern where shelf was removed)

**Scene 4**
    As before, with:
        Jack's pistol and gunbelt
        Jack's apple
        Elmore's seven dollar bills
        Elmore's silver-backed mirror wrapped in white cloth
            with blue border (for Bess)
        Bess's hat and shoes (brought on from R. by Macon)

**Scene 5**
    Bench and chair as before
    For Jack — tray with pitcher of pink lemonade (with cut-
        up fruit floating)
    With Jack from inside cabin — one wooden chair with 2
        sofa cushions from Act II, Scene 1
    Will's long rifle
    Will's 2 slaughtering knives
    Will's dusty bullwhip
    Large burlap sack stuffed with wheat (Macon)

Bess' parasol
Elmore's leatherbound notepad and period pencil

**Scene 6**
Yard and cabin sets as before
Worktable — basket of cornbread, mason jar with water, carving knife, rag
Will's table — tablecloth as before, anchoring bowl, Bess' hat and gloves
Side table — lace cover, inkwell, steel pen
On sofa, Emore's folio with Boucicault letter, invitation, contract, illustration of Bess, list of sales, period newspaper, check for Bess
Coat pegs — dressing cape, white cape for Bess
3 pieces of luggage for Jack to carry
Will's long rifle and leather shoulder satchel
Repeat Will's glass eye and backup
Handrolled cigarette for Will

**Scene 7**
Chaise lounge
Plush rug
Standing ashtray
Pictures in gilt frames, curtains, sconce
Elmore's new portfolio with final contract, St. Louis *Chronicle*
Bess' filled whiskey glass
Jack's lit cigar and comic paper

**Scene 8**
Rough wooden camp table
Chair
Crate
On table — playing cards (set up for solitaire game in progress), whiskey bottle, tin mug, 2 handrolled cigarettes, ashtray
Lantern (circuited) hanging on tent pole

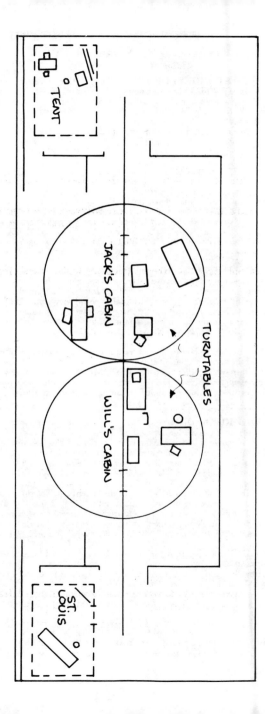

SCENE DESIGN
"ABUNDANCE"
~ DESIGNED BY ADRIANNE LOBEL
FOR MANHATTAN THEATRE CLUB

# NEW PLAYS

★ **AS BEES IN HONEY DROWN by Douglas Carter Beane.** Winner of the John Gassner Playwriting Award. A hot young novelist finds the subject of his new screenplay in a New York socialite who leads him into the world of *Auntie Mame* and *Breakfast at Tiffany's*, before she takes him for a ride. "A delicious soufflé of a satire ... [an] extremely entertaining fable for an age that always chooses image over substance." *–The NY Times* "... A witty assessment of one of the most active and relentless industries in a consumer society ... the creation of 'hot' young things, which the media have learned to mass produce with efficiency and zeal." *–The NY Daily News* [3M, 3W, flexible casting] ISBN: 0-8222-1651-5

★ **STUPID KIDS by John C. Russell.** In rapid, highly stylized scenes, the story follows four high-school students as they make their way from first through eighth period and beyond, struggling with the fears, frustrations, and longings peculiar to youth. "In STUPID KIDS ... playwright John C. Russell gets the opera of adolescence to a T ... The stylized teenspeak of STUPID KIDS ... suggests that Mr. Russell may have hidden a tape recorder under a desk in study hall somewhere and then scoured the tapes for good quotations ... it is the kids' insular, ceaselessly churning world, a pre-adult world of Doritos and libidos, that the playwright seeks to lay bare." *–The NY Times* "STUPID KIDS [is] a sharp-edged ... whoosh of teen angst and conformity anguish. It is also very funny." *–NY Newsday* [2M, 2W] ISBN: 0-8222-1698-1

★ **COLLECTED STORIES by Donald Margulies.** From Obie Award-winner Donald Margulies comes a provocative analysis of a student-teacher relationship that turns sour when the protégé becomes a rival. "With his fine ear for detail, Margulies creates an authentic, insular world, and he gives equal weight to the opposing viewpoints of two formidable characters." *–The LA Times* "This is probably Margulies' best play to date ..." *–The NY Post* "... always fluid and lively, the play is thick with ideas, like a stock-pot of good stew." *–The Village Voice* [2W] ISBN: 0-8222-1640-X

★ **FREEDOMLAND by Amy Freed.** An overdue showdown between a son and his father sets off fireworks that illuminate the neurosis, rage and anxiety of one family – and of America at the turn of the millennium. "FREEDOMLAND's more obvious links are to *Buried Child* and *Bosoms and Neglect*. Freed, like Guare, is an inspired wordsmith with a gift for surreal touches in situations grounded in familiar and real territory." *–Curtain Up* [3M, 4W] ISBN: 0-8222-1719-8

★ **STOP KISS by Diana Son.** A poignant and funny play about the ways, both sudden and slow, that lives can change irrevocably. "There's so much that is vital and exciting about STOP KISS ... you want to embrace this young author and cheer her onto other works ... the writing on display here is funny and credible ... you also will be charmed by its heartfelt characters and up-to-the-minute humor." *–The NY Daily News* "... irresistibly exciting ... a sweet, sad, and enchantingly sincere play." *–The NY Times* [3M, 3W] ISBN: 0-8222-1731-7

★ **THREE DAYS OF RAIN by Richard Greenberg.** The sins of fathers and mothers make for a bittersweet elegy in this poignant and revealing drama. "... a work so perfectly judged it heralds the arrival of a major playwright ... Greenberg is extraordinary." *–The NY Daily News* "Greenberg's play is filled with graceful passages that are by turns melancholy, harrowing, and often, quite funny." *–Variety* [2M, 1W] ISBN: 0-8222-1676-0

★ **THE WEIR by Conor McPherson.** In a bar in rural Ireland, the local men swap spooky stories in an attempt to impress a young woman from Dublin who recently moved into a nearby "haunted" house. However, the tables are soon turned when she spins a yarn of her own. "You shed all sense of time at this beautiful and devious new play." *–The NY Times* "Sheer theatrical magic. I have rarely been so convinced that I have just seen a modern classic. Tremendous." *–The London Daily Telegraph* [4M, 1W] ISBN: 0-8222-1706-6

**DRAMATISTS PLAY SERVICE, INC.**
**440 Park Avenue South, New York, NY 10016  212-683-8960  Fax 212-213-1539**
**postmaster@dramatists.com   www.dramatists.com**